INCLUSIVE CITIES
URBAN AREA GUIDELINES

MARCH 2022

ADB

ASIAN DEVELOPMENT BANK

CONTENTS

TABLES, FIGURES, AND BOXES

Tables

Figures

Boxes

FOREWORD

The Asian Development Bank (ADB) Strategy 2030 notes that ADB will promote quality infrastructure investments that are green, sustainable, resilient, and inclusive. Making cities livable is a key operational priority. With longer life expectancies and decreased fertility rates, rapid aging in Asia and the Pacific has put the region at the forefront of one of the most important global demographic trends. By 2050, one in four people in Asia and the Pacific will be over 60 years old. The Sustainable Development Goals 2030 Agenda recognizes that disability inclusion must be at the heart of poverty eradication. Through its infrastructure operations, ADB seeks to improve access of the poor, women, and vulnerable groups, especially the elderly and persons with disabilities (PWDs), to urban infrastructure and services to improve their quality of life.

ADB will continue to work with developing member countries to strengthen social protection systems and service delivery for those in need. Social protection elements will be integrated into projects in the urban sector to address age-friendly, gender-sensitive, and disability-supportive infrastructure. An important aspect of this is to ensure a seamless and accessible built environment. When a city is not accessible for PWDs, it infringes on their human rights and limits access to opportunities such as employment and education.

Inclusive Cities: Urban Area Guidelines is the first of its kind, prepared to support the development of inclusive cities that are accessible for all. Initially driven by the accessible tourism agenda in Georgia, the guidelines have evolved to provide guidance on inclusive city design and the implementation of universal standards applicable to Georgia.

Inclusive city design and the implementation of universal design standards are now widely recognized as essential and not just a good practice. The recent impact of the global pandemic, coronavirus disease 2019 (COVID-19), has further emphasized the need for inclusive cities. Given the changed habits regarding work, education, and social interaction, a city built to embrace diversity and accommodate the needs of the marginalized, especially persons with disabilities and the elderly, can and will benefit society as a whole. These guidelines, initiated in 2017, were prepared through a participatory approach and have contributed to national level reforms, evidenced by the Government of Georgia's approval of the Georgian National Accessibility Standard in December 2020. The guidelines are based on the approved standard and cover the wider topic and international practices focusing on inclusive cities development.

Chapter 1 of the guidelines provides the context and rationale for inclusive design. Chapter 2 sets out the social and policy context, which emphasizes that the creation of inclusive cities is essential for long-term sustainability and viability. It also highlights the importance of genuine engagement with end users in urban design, planning, and development. Chapter 3 provides Georgia's parliamentary-approved national accessibility standards. These are technical international standards with diagrams that will support architects, designers, urban planners, developers, and other professionals engaged in creating city infrastructure and buildings. In Chapter 4, the technical standards are supplemented with case studies demonstrating how these standards can be realized in practice. The case studies of inclusive city design initiatives globally, across Europe and Georgia, are a rich source of inspiration and practical examples. A case study on the first nonsovereign affordable housing project incorporating these guidelines into its design showcases a strong market demonstration and is expected to catalyze more private investment for a more livable city.

Inclusive Cities: Urban Area Guidelines aims to support capacity building and delivery of more inclusive design outcomes, and ultimately create more inclusive cities that will benefit everyone now and in the future. Without effective implementation, change will not take place, thus applying these guidelines and technical standards into public and private sector projects is critical in achieving a city for all.

We hope that these guidelines serve as an important policy tool to support the Government of Georgia in developing inclusive, accessible, and livable cities. The guidelines are an outcome of extensive consultations with stakeholders—government and citizens—who provided valuable feedback and insights. These are relevant for replication across the wider Central and West Asia region and other ADB developing member countries.

ADB will continue to help its developing member countries in identifying new and effective mechanisms in making cities more livable—one of the key operational priorities of ADB Strategy 2030.

YEVGENIY ZHUKOV
Director General
Central and West Asia Department
Asian Development Bank

ACKNOWLEDGMENTS

Inclusive Cities: Urban Area Guidelines has been produced as part of ADB's technical assistance on *Livable Urban Areas: Integrated Urban Plans for Balanced Regional Development* in Georgia. Ramola Naik Singru, principal urban development specialist, Urban Development and Water Division (CWUW), Central and West Asia Department (CWRD), led the technical assistance and guided the preparation of these guidelines. South Asia Department's (SARD) urban development specialist Laxmi Sharma and CWUW young professional Xijie Lu, and ADB Georgia Resident Mission's (GRM) associate project officer (infrastructure) Tea Papuashvili jointly supervised the technical assistance and the preparation of these guidelines.

David Bazashvili, Nana Chartolani, and Tamar Makharashvili of the Accessible Tourism Centre (PARSA) drafted the guidelines. Among those who provided inputs are Ivor Ambrose and Katerina Papamichail of the European Network for Accessible Tourism (ENAT), and Giorgi Gabidauri, Marina Mchedlishvili, Inga Sharikadze, and Giga Sopromadze of Tbilisi City Hall. The project team coordinated with the technical assistance consultants that prepared the Integrated Urban Action Plans led by Neils van Dijk and Ian Hamilton from OTAK Inc., and with the Regional Environmental Centre for the Caucasus led by Sophiko Akhobadze.

Iain McKinnon and Mikaela Patrick of the Global Disability Innovation Hub (GDI Hub) reviewed, consolidated, and finalized the guidelines considering global best practice and application of an inclusive approach.

The project team would like to thank the following for their support and endorsement of the guidelines: Ministry of Regional Development and Infrastructure of Georgia, Ministry of Finance of Georgia, Human Rights Secretariat under the President of Georgia, Ministry of Economy and Sustainable Development, Municipal Development Fund of Georgia, Tbilisi City Hall, Tbilisi City Assembly, Georgia National Tourism Administration, and National Statistics Office of Georgia. The valuable inputs in the assessment preparation provided by the participants of the stakeholder workshops held in Georgia are greatly appreciated.

The guidelines were prepared in a participatory manner through consultation workshops involving stakeholders from the central government ministries, local governments, development partners, and civil society. Analyses were done using secondary data review and discussions with relevant agencies. The team is especially grateful to the guidance provided by Mzia Giorgobiani, Deputy Minister, Ministry of Regional Development and Infrastructure of Georgia; Nikoloz Gagua, Deputy Minister of Finance; Yong Ye, country director, ADB-Pakistan Resident Mission; Yesim M. Elhan-Kayalar, country director (until August 2019), ADB-GRM; and Shane Rosenthal, country director, ADB-GRM (since September 2019).

The following provided valuable peer review: Stephane Bessadi, senior water utility specialist, Procurement, Portfolio, and Financial Management Department (PPFD); Neil Chadder, project manager, Cities Development Initiative for Asia (CDIA); Sonia Chand Sandhu, senior advisor to the Vice-President for Knowledge Management (until 2019); Sushma Kotagiri, principal facilitation specialist (accountability mechanism) (until 2020), Office of the Special Project Facilitator (until July 2020); Joanna Rogers, social development consultant (disability), Social Development Thematic Group, Sustainable Development and Climate Change Department (SDCC); Mary Alice G. Rosero, senior social development specialist (gender and development), Portfolio, Results, Safeguards and Gender Unit, CWRD; and Lloyd Wright, senior urban development specialist (transport), CWUW.

The following coordinated the production and publication of these guidelines: CWRD-CWUW's senior project officer Carina T. Soliman, project analyst Liza Jane Domingo, senior operations assistant Gina Sinang, knowledge products coordinator consultant Vince Docta, cover design artist Claudette Rodrigo, graphic artist Gato Borrero, and ADB Department of Communications associate communications coordinator April-Marie Gallega.

AUTHORS AND CONTRIBUTORS

Authors

- Ramola Naik Singru, principal urban development specialist, ADB
- Xijie Lu, young professional, ADB
- Tamar Makharashvili, Accessible Tourism Centre (PARSA)
- David Bazashvili, PARSA
- Iain McKinnon, Global Disability Innovation Hub (GDI Hub)
- Mikaela Patrick, GDI Hub

Experts

- Laxmi Sharma, senior urban development specialist, ADB
- Tea Papuashvili, project officer, ADB
- Nana Chartolani, PARSA
- Ivor Ambrose, European Network for Accessible Tourism (ENAT)
- Katerina Papamichail, ENAT

Publication coordinators

- Carina Soliman, senior project officer, ADB
- Liza Jane Domingo, project analyst, ADB
- Gina Sinang, senior operations assistant, ADB
- April-Marie Gallega, associate communications coordinator, ADB
- Vince Docta, knowledge products coordinator consultant, ADB

ABBREVIATIONS

ADB	Asian Development Bank
CRPD	Convention on the Rights of Persons with Disabilities
CWRD	Central and West Asia Department, ADB
CWUW	Urban Development and Water Division, ADB
DMC	developing member country
ENAT	European Network for Accessible Tourism
EU	European Union
ICC	International Code Council
mm	millimeter
MRDI	Ministry of Regional Development and Infrastructure of Georgia
NGO	nongovernment organization
OECD	Organisation for Economic Co-operation and Development
PARSA	Georgia's Accessible Tourism Centre
PWDs	persons with disabilities
SDG	Sustainable Development Goal
UK	United Kingdom
UN	United Nations
UNCRPD	United Nations Convention on the Rights of Persons with Disabilities
WHO	World Health Organization

EXECUTIVE SUMMARY

The Asian Development Bank (ADB) has long been advocating the importance of creating inclusive cities. Since 2008, ADB's Strategy has focused on inclusive development and livable cities. *Asia 2050: Realizing the Asian Century* focuses on making cities more inclusive and ensuring people who need support have access to the services they need to better their quality of life. The ADB Strategy 2030 identifies making cities more livable as one of its seven operational priorities to support the transformation of developing cities in the Asia and Pacific region into safe, inclusive, and sustainable urban centers.

ADB publication on *Enabling Inclusive Cities: Tool Kit for Inclusive Urban Development* (2017) defines an inclusive city as "a safe, livable environment with affordable and equitable access to urban services, social services, and livelihood opportunities for all the city residents and other city users to promote optimal development of its human capital and ensure the respect of human dignity and equality."

The need for more inclusive cities is recognized globally with more than half of the world's population now living in urban settlements. The Asia and Pacific region remains one of the top urbanizing continents in the world, second to Africa, with its urban population projected to reach 3 billion by 2050. This urbanization is not always accompanied by equivalent infrastructure development, leading to wide gaps in urban equality.

The global demand from persons with disabilities (PWDs) is also better understood. It is estimated that nearly 1 billion people, or 15% of the global population, experience some form of disability, and its prevalence is higher in developing countries. One-fifth of the estimated global total, or between 110 million and 190 million people, experience significant disabilities. More than half of Georgia's population is urban (53.7%), half of which is in the capital city, Tbilisi, which is also home to 20% of Georgia's population of PWDs. Evidence also suggests that there are demographic disparities between rural and urban populations. Young people migrate to the city, leaving behind aging rural populations and thus creating challenges to inclusive development.

The confluence of these two global trends has resulted in many PWDs living in poverty in urban areas where barriers to equitable access exist. While this presents significant and often complex challenges, there are opportunities. In the case of infrastructure development, there is an opportunity to ensure it delivers universal design solutions that provide greater accessibility and usability of the built environment, not just to support PWDs, but also to create safer, more inclusive, and livable cities that work better for everyone.

Adopting and implementing a universal design approach can deliver intuitive and more elegant solutions that work better and provide more positive user experiences, regardless of ability or support need. This can, in turn, help eliminate the need for future alterations, add-ons, operational support, mitigation, and compensation. It will also ensure what is being delivered from the outset is genuinely fit for purpose in a sustainable way.

The inclusive cities guidelines aim to support designers and decision-makers responsible for creating and delivering new infrastructure developments in Georgia to ensure they contribute toward the creation of inclusive and livable cities. These guidelines set out the current social and policy context, highlights the universal design technical standards to be applied in practice, and presents case studies and good examples to inform and inspire policy makers and practitioners across Georgia and internationally.

Using the principles of universal design to help deliver more inclusive and livable cities does not just support a niche market segment. It also creates sustainable solutions wherein everybody will benefit for a lifetime.

Universal design in practice. Visitors to Queen Elizabeth Olympic Park use an external passenger lift in east London, United Kingdom (photo by Iain Mckinnon).

1 INTRODUCTION

Inclusive Cities: Urban Area Guidelines aims to support government officials, urban planners, architects, developers, and service delivery providers in the urban development and tourism sectors and beyond, in understanding the value of and in delivering accessible built environment, places, and services.

Inclusive cities support the urban population by creating more welcoming and intuitive places that help increase the quality of life and create a more positive experience of the built environment and public spaces for everyone. This is especially important in supporting a vibrant and dynamic tourism industry, which is a key revenue generator for Georgia and other countries in Central and West Asia.

Inclusive cities address the needs of persons with disabilities (PWDs) ensuring equal access to all urban services.[1] ADB's developing member countries (DMCs) should be increasingly aware of the needs of PWDs and the elderly.[2] The inclusive urban area guidelines will help create a barrier-free, accessible, and inclusive city with a better quality of life for all its inhabitants, including PWDs, the elderly, women, and children. Though the focus is on Georgia, the guidelines are also relevant to all countries in the Central and West Asia region and the wider DMCs moving toward the creation of inclusive cities through the adoption and implementation of universal design practice.

Policies pertaining to access to education, employment, urban services, and the built environment are still in their nascent stage in most developing countries. Hence, it is important to draw from the learning experience of progressive nations to create an inclusive built environment that supports all members of society, regardless of ability, age, sex, or religion.

Tourism is a fast growing industry and a key driver of Georgia's economic growth, accounting for 26.3% of the country's gross domestic product in 2019. Tourism is an important source of employment, contributing to 27.7% of total employment in 2019 in Georgia, the highest in the Central and West Asia region. International visitors increased by 345% between 2010 and 2019 and totaled about 7.7 million in 2019, generating $3.2 billion in receipts. The majority of trips (76.3% or 5.5 million) were from neighboring countries, while only 23.7% (1.7 million) were from other countries. Despite a high number

---

[1] ADB's Urban Sector Group–Inclusive Cities Working Group developed the definition of inclusive cities. Services include water supply, sanitation, solid waste management, housing, and transport facilities; social services are typically health, education, culture, and public space. Stakeholders are government, communities, civil society, and the private sector. Social protection includes systems for upholding the rights of children, youth, women, the elderly, and indigenous peoples.

[2] R. Naik Singru and M. Lindfield. 2017. *Enabling Inclusive Cities: Tool Kit for Inclusive Urban Development.* Manila: Asian Development Bank.

of visitors, associated tourism revenues lag behind. The low visitor spending is a result of a shortage of high-quality tourism experiences and the skills deficiencies to manage and market the tourism assets.

The Georgia National Tourism Strategy 2025 aims to create unique, high-quality visitor experiences based on the country's inherent natural and cultural assets. Despite a promising prospect, basic urban services and associated tourism infrastructure in Georgia have become outdated and are only partially functioning. Integrated investments in inclusive urban services and accessible tourism infrastructure will significantly improve not only the visitor experience for tourists, but also the livability for all citizens including PWDs, the elderly, women, and families with young children. In doing so, Georgia will be well placed to meet the needs of its citizens and the increasing demand for quality tourism, unlocking the economic potential of its towns and cities.[3]

Urban Planning Context

People's daily functioning and well-being greatly depend on the quality and sustainability of the infrastructure they live and work in. Such infrastructure is important for ensuring equal opportunities and easy access to public services for all the citizens, regardless of their abilities, gender, and age.

In tackling Georgia's contemporary built environment and urban planning, it is necessary to consider the existing heritage of Soviet city planning. Soviet architecture provided limited support to children, women, PWDs, and other marginalized groups.[4] Some groups were marginalized to the extent of criminal prosecution, while others, such as children with disabilities, remained under permanent threat of institutionalization. Gender equality was mostly limited to labor rights, often sidelining other human rights.[5] Moreover, the notion of mainstreaming equality for all was eliminated from the needs list. There was no demand for services for women, sexual minorities, children, and PWDs because of the legislative, environmental, physical, and attitudinal regulations that existed for much of the 20th century. These had a significant impact on the design of Georgia's post-Soviet urban infrastructure.

Ensuring accessibility of existing facilities and services as well as introducing inclusive services and environments will contribute to the inclusion of PWDs, the elderly, women, and children in society. These developments will allow them to exercise their fundamental human rights, providing access to equal opportunities and participation for all.

Universal Design

An inclusive environment is the first step toward fulfilling the rights of PWDs to participate in all areas of community life. One way to help achieve this is by introducing universal design standards. According to a report by the United Kingdom's Department for International Development, inclusive design

---

[3]   ADB. 2020. *Proposed Loan to the Government of Georgia: Livable Cities Investment Program (LCIP) for Balanced Development.* Concept Paper. Manila.

[4]   S. D. Philips. 2020. There Are No Invalids in the USSR: A Missing Chapter in New Disability History. *Disability Studies Quarterly.* 29 (3).

[5]   Infrastructure and Cities for Economic Development (ICED). *Delivering Disability Inclusive Infrastructure in Low Income Countries.*

of the built environment through universal design is one of the six priority areas for infrastructure development that is inclusive of PWDs (footnote 5).

The definition of standards and approaches for an inclusive built environment varies globally—from universal design to inclusive design to design for all. However, what they all have in common is they go beyond the minimum technical standards for accessibility. While an accessible environment might provide step-free access, a genuinely inclusive environment will provide equality of experience for everyone.

Inclusive environments embrace diversity and flexibility, understanding that everyone has different needs, and those needs are constantly changing.[6] The way in which an inclusively designed built environment can embrace and celebrate different cultures has huge potential for growing an inclusive tourism sector.[7]

To effectively deliver inclusive environments, implementing universal design and accessibility standards from the beginning of new construction projects is essential. It is much more cost-effective to introduce these measures during the planning and design stage, where the added cost of integrating accessibility requirements is far less (typically 1% or less of the total construction budget) than when applied later in the design process, and during or after construction.[8] For cities that depend on tourism and aim to attract more visitors, considering that inaccessible environments contribute to a decrease in global market share of 15%–20%, the economic advantage of early and strategic application of universal design standards is clear.[9]

Accessible Tourism

Striving for the economic development of its regions, the Government of Georgia places high priority on conserving and protecting cultural and historical heritage and improving employment and livelihood opportunities for the local population through the development of tourism infrastructure.

The government pays particular attention to the possibilities that accessible tourism development can bring to the country. Accessible tourism is one of the important driving forces for the development of cities in accordance with the UN's Sustainable Development Goals (SDGs), and in particular, SDG 11 (Make cities and human settlements inclusive, safe, resilient, and sustainable). Accessibility and sustainable mobility, a diverse and resilient local economy, vibrant public spaces, and affordability are some of the fundamental aspects of livable cities. By 2050, it is expected that about 6.25 billion of the world's population, 15% of them PWDs, will be living in urban areas.[10] Inclusive and sustainable

---

6   Global Disability Innovation Hub, Queen Elizabeth Olympic Park, and London Legacy Development Corporation. *Inclusive Design Standards.*

7   Asian Development Bank. 2016. *Realizing the Urban Potential in Georgia: National Urban Assessment.* Executive Summary. Manila. https://www.adb.org/sites/default/files/institutional-document/186168/urban-potential-georgia-exec-sum.pdf.

8   WHO. 2011. *World Report on Disability.* Geneva.

9   European Commission. 2014. Economic Impact and Travel Patterns of Accessible Tourism in Europe. Final Report. https://www.un.org/disabilities/documents/sdgs/disability_inclusive_sdgs.pdf.

10 United Nations Enable. 2016. Disability and Sustainable Urban Development. http://www.un.org/disabilities/documents/accessible_urban_dev_infographic.pdf.

urban development planning, therefore, ensures full and active inclusion of PWDs, the elderly, women, and children.

Restored travel destinations, ancient cities, health resorts, and newly constructed hotels and concert halls are already popular with thousands of inbound tourists across Georgia. However, a significant opportunity remains to sustainably increase the number of visitors by making these travel destinations accessible for all. Although Georgia has already taken important steps to protect the rights of PWDs, many tourist destinations do not yet support visitors with disabilities. Tourism sector personnel also require appropriate awareness education and skills training in regard to disability equality. The development of inclusive services for all customers will help protect their human rights and further support the creation of accessible environments.

Accessible tourism and universal design are integral to the philosophy of independent living for PWDs and other individuals with specific access needs. The application of these approaches will enable them to participate in tourism and civil activities and cultural life of society. Universal design helps remove barriers and increase participation, which in turn reduces stigma. Evidence shows that PWDs associate the inaccessibility of infrastructure and services with the experience of stigma,[11] highlighting the importance of designing an inclusive physical environment.

International Context

Equality of access and mobility are concepts set out in international agreements. Every person, regardless of their physical, cognitive, or sensory impairment, should have an equal right to enjoy barrier-free mobility and travel services. This right was specified by the United Nations General Assembly in the Convention on the Rights of Persons with Disabilities (UNCRPD), adopted on 13 December 2006 and signed by 163 countries, including Georgia.[12] Georgia ratified the Convention and it officially came into force on 12 April 2014. Article 30 of the Convention refers to ensuring the right to equal opportunity to participate in leisure, tourism, and sports.[13]

The Association Agreement between Georgia and the European Union (EU) was signed and ratified in 2014 and includes a deep and comprehensive free trade agreement.[14] The Association Agreement includes "cooperation in the field of tourism, with the aim of strengthening the development of a competitive and sustainable tourism industry as a generator of economic growth and empowerment, employment and international exchange." This highlights the importance of fostering more inclusive labor markets and social systems that integrate disadvantaged people, including PWDs and people from other minority groups.

---

[11]   M. Patrick, I. McKinnon, and V. Austin. 2020. Inclusive Design and Accessibility in Ulaanbaatar, Mongolia. *AT2030 Inclusive Infrastructure Case Studies.* Prepared by the Global Disability Innovation Hub and partners for the UK Foreign, Commonwealth and Development Office. DOI: 10.13140/RG.2.2.26922.44485.

[12]   In addition to the 163 signatories, there were 181 ratifications or accessions, and for the Optional Protocol, there were 96 ratifications or accessions and 94 signatories. See United Nations Department of Economic and Social Affairs. Convention on the Rights of Persons with Disabilities (CRPD).

[13]   United Nations Human Rights Office of the High Commissioner. Convention on the Rights of Persons with Disabilities. https://www.ohchr.org/EN/HRBodies/CRPD/Pages/ConventionRightsPersonsWithDisabilities.aspx.

[14]   European Commission. Georgia. https://ec.europa.eu/trade/policy/countries-and-regions/countries/georgia/.

Figure 1: Strategic Context and Regulatory Framework

- International convention(s)
- National equality law(s)
- National building regulations
- National universal design guidelines
- Implementation
- Inclusive urban development
- Accessible cities for all
- Disability equality and awareness education or training for frontline staff
- Accessible tourism
- More accessible service for everyone
- Economic benefits due to increased use of services and larger tourism market

Source: Asian Development Bank.

2 SOCIAL AND POLICY CONTEXT

Inclusive Urban Development

Creating Cities for All

An inclusive built environment and accessible tourism in Georgia requires all sectors and stakeholders to mainstream equality for all groups that experience exclusion, including persons with disabilities (PWDs), women, children, the elderly, as well as sexual, religious, and other minorities. Mainstreaming equality means creating cities for all, cities that are inclusive and represent human dignity and equality. Cities should demonstrate leadership in progress toward inclusion; and inclusive city frameworks complemented by universal design approaches and practical guidelines can support this.

The Disability Inclusive and Accessible Urban Development Network (DIAUD), World Enabled, and Christian Blind Mission (CBM) define an inclusive city as "a place where everyone, regardless of their economic means, gender, ethnicity, disability, age or religion, is enabled and empowered to fully participate in the social, economic, cultural and political opportunities that cities have to offer."[15]

"Inclusive cities" is a major policy focus for achieving the SDGs. As the global population continues to urbanize, cities are becoming more instrumental centers for sustainable development. Urbanization has historically been considered a cause of poverty and exclusion, with an increasing urban population linked to rising inequality. Evidence shows that inequality in cities is rising.[16] Habitat III and the launch of the New Urban Agenda represented a policy shift toward thinking about the opportunities offered in and by cities rather than focusing on the barriers and challenges. "Inclusive cities" is one of the agendas that represents this focus toward engaging and involving historically excluded groups in decision-making that shapes the cities they live in.[17]

Inclusive cities require commitment and vision by all stakeholders that play a role in shaping the built environment including

---

[15] Disability Inclusive and Accessible Urban Development Network (DIAUD), World Enabled, and CBM. 2016. The Inclusion Imperative: Towards Disability-Inclusive and Accessible Urban Development. *Key Recommendations for an Inclusive Urban Agenda*. p. 13.

[16] UN Habitat. Inclusive, Vibrant Neighbourhoods and Communities. https://unhabitat.org/programme/inclusive-vibrant-neighbourhoods-and-communities (accessed 19 September 2020).

[17] R. Naik Singru and M. Lindfield. 2017. *Enabling Inclusive Cities: Tool Kit for Inclusive Urban Development*. Manila: Asian Development Bank; World Bank. *World Inclusive Cities Approach Paper*. https://documents1.worldbank.org/curated/en/402451468169453117/pdf/AUS8539-REVISED-WP-P148654-PUBLIC-Box393236B-Inclusive-Cities-Approach-Paper-w-Annexes-final.pdf. D.C. Mitlin and D. Satterthwaite. 2016. *On the Engagement of Excluded Groups in Inclusive Cities: Highlighting Good Practices and Key Challenges in the Global South*. Urban Development Series Knowledge Papers. Washington, DC: World Bank.

- government stakeholders who shape policies and decisions on infrastructure,
- urban planning and built environment professionals,
- service providers and human rights champions,
- industry stakeholders who fund and deliver projects, and
- community stakeholders—the people who benefit most from a more inclusive city.

Early and strategic commitment to inclusive city making is essential. Integrating the voices of those who experience the most inequity in the built environment, such as the PWDs, early on in planning and design processes is equally important. When these voices are neglected until later stages, such as in post-construction audits, accommodations and changes to meet accessibility standards will be more expensive and less likely to be realized (footnote 13).

Creating and enabling inclusive cities requires an integrated and multisector approach. ADB's Enabling Inclusive Cities Tool Kit suggests the following areas of intervention:

- joint strategic visions of all stakeholders through a participatory planning and decision-making process incorporating universal design, integrated urban planning, transparent accountability mechanisms, and the use of the city's inherent assets;
- knowledge and information sharing;
- public participation and contribution;
- mechanisms, such as cross-subsidies, social protection, and gender balance, to ensure an adequate standard of living to the most economically disadvantaged and vulnerable population;
- geographical and social mobility;
- business environment and pro-poor financing services that attract capital investment and enable everybody to undertake economic activities;
- resilience to global, environmental, and socioeconomic shocks and threats; and
- mechanisms to ensure the sustainable use of a city's resources (footnote 3).

The following sections describe key thematic areas for creating cities for all, localizing efforts toward the SDGs, and integrating universal design approaches to these different thematic areas.

Localizing the United Nations Sustainable Development Goals (SDGs) for Inclusive Urban Development in Georgia

The driving international framework behind inclusive and sustainable development is the United Nations (UN) Sustainable Development Goals (SDGs). The SDGs are a universal set of global goals for a better and more sustainable future for all, to be achieved by 2030.[18] To achieve these global societal goals considering areas such as economic growth, employment creation, environmental sustainability, and well-being, a focus should be placed on an integrated policy approach to quality and sustainable infrastructure development.

---

[18]   United Nations Sustainable Development Goals. https://www.un.org/sustainabledevelopment/sustainable-development-goals/.

Figure 2: Overview of the Sustainable Development Goals

Source: United Nations, Department of Economic and Social Affairs. Sustainable Development. The 17 Goals. https://sdgs.un.org/goals.

In Georgia, considerable efforts have been undertaken to achieve the SDGs. The government has identified 13 out of 17 SDG targets that are of particular national interest. Strong national commitment to the SDGs is accompanied by an inclusive participation approach, public awareness raising, and monitoring and evaluation strategies.[19] One lesson learned from the Millennium Development Goals is that local governments lack the capacity to meet SDG targets. With this in view, ADB supports its developing member countries, including Georgia, in localizing plans to achieve the SDGs.[20]

The ADB 2030 Strategy advocates for a series of operational pillars to realize prosperous, inclusive, resilient, and sustainable development in Asia and the Pacific. Given the size of this region's population, it is instrumental in the success of the SDGs. Issues such as infrastructure deficits, rapid urbanization, and demographic changes pose challenges which ADB seeks to address through country-focused approaches that promote innovative technology and deliver integrated solutions. Livable and inclusive cities is one of ADB's seven operational priority areas that these guidelines contribute to.

---

[19]   United Nations Sustainable Development Group. 2016. The Sustainable Development Goals are Coming to Life: Stories of Country Implementation and UN Support. https://unsdg.un.org/resources/sustainable-development-goals-are-coming-life-stories-country-implementation-and-un.

[20]   Asian Development Bank. 2019. *Strategy 2030 Operational Plan for Priority 4: Making Cities More Livable, 2019–2024*. Manila.

Applying the universal design and inclusive planning processes can support the creation of safe, healthy urban environments and inclusive cities with access to social services that directly targets the urban poor and seeks to lessen inequality (footnote 1). In Georgia, more gender inclusive urban environments are being created through economic, transport, and urban planning sector activities such as the development of "Fair Shared City Guidelines."[21] A comprehensive universal design approach can address barriers to inclusion across different domains such as age, gender, and disability (this will be discussed in Chapter 2.3). This requires strategic vision and early planning to ensure universal design measures are implemented as effectively as possible, maximizing the benefits for people experiencing inequality.

Georgia experiences social development and inclusion challenges which constrain the country from meeting the SDGs.

Income inequality. Since 2015, Georgia has experienced both reduction in poverty (by 7%) and economic growth (an annual average growth rate of 4.1%). To date, income inequality and inclusive economic growth are still major challenges. Globally, income inequality is rising, and it disproportionately affects excluded groups such as women and PWDs. Women spend double the amount of time on unpaid labor compared to men. PWDs are more likely to be unemployed and have higher healthcare costs.

Inclusive economic growth. The SDGs offer an important framework for policy making in Georgia toward inclusive and multidimensional economic growth. The annual growth rate of the tourism sector between 2015 and 2019 was 10%. Due to this growth rate, the tourism, agriculture, and manufacturing sectors are considered important opportunity areas for inclusive growth. Work is ongoing to alleviate gender inequality, discrimination, and health and safety issues in Georgia's labor market through the adoption of European Union (EU) Directives in the EU-Georgia Association Agreement. Furthermore, the Government of Georgia is supporting tertiary education and vocational training for the disadvantaged groups such as ethnic minorities and PWDs.[22] Unemployment for PWDs is high at 65.6% in 2014, significantly higher than that of Europe's average of 33.6%.[23]

Urban–rural disparity. Access to infrastructure, opportunity, and prosperity is not equal across Georgia. The country has profound urban to rural disparity. More than half of Georgia's population is urban (53.7%), half of which is in the capital city, Tbilisi, and the rest are spread across smaller urban settlements (footnote 7). Young people migrate to the city, leaving an older population in rural areas, hence creating a reliance on a "proactive older workforce" for agricultural productivity. The gross domestic product (GDP) per capita in Tbilisi is nearly double the rest of the country, and triple that of

---

[21] ADB. 2020. *Knowledge and Support Technical Assistance (KSTA): Georgia—Strengthening Local Institutions to Plan and Design Gender Responsive and Inclusive Urban Development. Future Cities Future Women (Phase 2).* Subproject Proposal for Output 2 Allocation under TA 9387-REG: Strengthening Institutions for Localizing Agenda 2030 for Sustainable Development. Technical Report. Manila. ADB and Tbilisi City Municipality. 2021. Fair shared green and recreational spaces guidelines for gender-responsive and inclusive design. Manila. https://www.adb.org/publications/green-spaces-guidelines-gender-responsive-design-tbilisi.

[22] Administration of the Government of Georgia. 2020. *Georgia Voluntary National Review: Report on the Implementation of the 2030 Agenda on Sustainable Development.* https://sustainabledevelopment.un.org/content/documents/26390VNR_2020_Georgia_Report.pdf.

[23] Institute for the Development of Freedom of Information. 2018. *Data Analysis on Persons with Disabilities Living in Georgia.* https://idfi.ge/en/data_analysis%20_on_persons_with_disabilities_living_in_georgia.

the poorest regions. Georgia is developing policies to address such spatial inequality such as the Law on the Development of the High Mountain regions, which seeks to regenerate essential infrastructure and services, preserve the country's cultural heritage, and modernize the tourism infrastructure (footnote 22). To create more inclusive cities across Georgia, initiatives should include investment in decentralized approaches to develop smaller urban centers and investment in initiatives such as cultural and agricultural tourism that would provide benefits across diverse sectors (footnote 2).

Unequal access to water and sanitation. Lack of clean water particularly affects women. Traditionally, they are mainly responsible for family hygiene and sanitation. In Georgia, these resources are generally available in urban areas, although the quality is variable. Furthermore, intensive urbanization risks undermine the drinking water access in Georgia's cities. In this example, challenges related to SDGs 5, 6, 9 and 11 intersect, indicating the importance of crosscutting and multisector approach.

Unequal energy access. Although all urban and rural areas in Georgia are connected to a 24-hour energy supply, not all Georgians can afford it. Obtaining cost-effective energy supply will require efficient international cooperation which, in turn, will necessitate expanding infrastructure and upgrading technologies. Creating equity in energy access through initiatives such as clean cooking facilities has the combined benefits of contributing to alleviating poverty and achieving the global climate goals. There are many benefits to achieving energy for all, primarily by tapping renewable energy sources. Increasing the share of renewables will help reduce household air pollution, prevent premature deaths, and mitigate carbon emissions. The International Energy Agency, together with the Clean Energy Education and Empowerment Technology Collaboration Program, works to strengthen the role of women in the clean energy sector. Removing barriers to women's active participation in sectors where they typically have been underrepresented, such as the clean energy sector, requires concrete actions in areas such as data collection and knowledge building, career development, awards programs, and dialogue.

Access to opportunities and participation in society. Ensuring social and economic interaction in society is the essence of urban settlement. Access to social and economic infrastructure, such as education, jobs, health services, childcare facilities, green commons, and cultural or religious institutions, can impact one's physical and mental health. The different social roles and physical needs of men and women require a consideration of gender when shaping cities and settlements. Particular attention must be paid to regional economic infrastructure to ensure equitable access for all.

Promoting inclusive and sustainable industrialization will significantly improve the participation of excluded groups in Georgia's economy. As an example, access to small and medium-sized industrial units and affordable financing mechanisms could be an enabling factor for women, decreasing inequality and increasing their level of independence. Supporting the development of domestic technology will support greater participation by women in the social and economic life of the country. While modern information and communication technologies are especially important for women and children, there is a large gap in development and success between those who have access and those who do not.

Persons with Disabilities

The inclusive city must be a disability inclusive city. An inclusively designed city for persons with disabilities (PWDs) has wider benefits for the whole population. For example, level access can make pedestrian movement easier for people using prams or pulling suitcases. Of Georgia's PWD population, 20% live in the capital, Tbilisi, making it an important region to lead by example in the inclusion and accessibility for PWDs in the built environment.[24]

The SDGs 2030 Agenda recognizes that disability inclusion must be at the heart of poverty eradication.[25] Article 9 of the United Nations Convention on the Rights of Persons with Disabilities (UNCRPD) explicitly connects access in the built environment to an inclusive society, stating that "Access to the physical environment, public transportation, knowledge, information and communication is a precondition for persons with disabilities to fulfill their rights in an inclusive society." The Global Disability Summit in 2018 was an important moment where commitments to embedding disability inclusion in the infrastructure sector were made.[26]

When a city is not accessible for PWDs, it infringes on their human rights and limits access to opportunities such as employment and education. This is evidenced by the vicious cycle of disability and poverty. Research on multidimensional poverty suggests that there is a "disability development gap" where rates of poverty in households with PWDs are higher in middle-income settings than in lower-income settings, indicating that attention to disability inclusion in middle-income countries is essential.[27]

The *World Report on Disability* identifies priority areas that create an enabling and accessible environment for PWDs:

- Accessibility policies and standards should meet the needs of all PWDs.
- Monitor and evaluate the implementation of accessibility laws and standards through an impartial body that includes significant representation of PWDs.
- Awareness raising is needed to address ignorance and prejudice around disability. Public-facing workers should receive training; wider education and awareness campaigns can support a culture of inclusion.
- Education and training on accessibility and inclusion should be mandatory for built environment training and education programs. Policy makers should also receive training on these issues (footnote 25).

[24] Institute for the Development of Freedom of Information. 2015. *Statistics of Persons with Disabilities in Georgia.* https://idfi.ge/en/statistics-of-persons-with-disabilities.

[25] World Health Organization and World Bank. 2011. *World Report on Disability 2011.* Geneva. https://www.who.int/disabilities/world_report/2011/report.pdf.

[26] Infrastructure and Cities for Economic Development (ICED). Delivering Disability Inclusive Infrastructure in Low Income Countries.

[27] M. Pinilla-Roncancio and S. Alkire. 2020. How Poor are People with Disabilities? Evidence Based on the Global Multidimensional Poverty Index. *Journal of Disability Policy Studies.* 17 May. https://doi.org/10.1177/1044207320919942.

International organizations can support such efforts through

- developing global accessibility standards for different domains of the physical environment that adapt to resource constraints, heritage, and cultural diversity;
- funding development projects that are contingent upon compliance to accessibility standards and the promotion of universal design;
- supporting research to evidence good practice and help form policies, with specific focus on lower-income settings;
- developing indices to provide reliable and consistent data on accessibility;
- promoting accessibility and universal design and mainstreaming its adoption; and
- involving PWDs and the disabled persons' organizations (DPOs).

The *World Report on Disability* also proposes three key areas of focus for an accessible physical environment:

- public accommodations such as buildings and roads,
- transportation, and
- information and communication.

These recommendations suggest that creating a disability-inclusive city is a combination of national and international efforts. A universal design approach requires a flexible and adaptive mindset. While the principles of accessibility and inclusion can be universal, the practical application of accessibility is context-specific and depends on local conditions such as culture, climate, geography, resources, capabilities, and knowledge. That is why country-specific guidelines, standards, and examples of good practice are necessary (footnote 13).

Gender Equality

Georgia has experienced intensive urbanization in recent decades, which has raised issues related to gender equality. Women are more active consumers of education, health, childcare, social services, and recreation. They are also significant contributors to urban infrastructure because of their role in caring for children and the elderly and their greater representation of employment in these sectors.

Infrastructure plays a central role as it supports the actions to deliver on the United Nations SDGs related to education, health, social protection, jobs, and the environment. To ensure gender equitable development of infrastructure, the location of services such as the design of public transport grids, and the frequency of transport must be planned through a gender lens.

Gender Mainstreaming

Gender mainstreaming is an approach to policy making that seeks to achieve gender equality by recognizing and addressing the needs of both men and women. A gender mainstreaming approach emphasizes reshaping mainstream attitudes, institutions, behaviors, and processes. This is achieved through analysis, advocacy, networking, results-based project management, and high-quality information management and communication. It requires that gender equality considerations are integrated into projects in all themes and sectors related to inclusive urban development. Where appropriate, gender mainstreaming should specifically target women or men, provided that the intention is to change mainstream thinking and action so that gender equality is achieved.

The Organisation of Economic Co-operation and Development (OECD) has incorporated three major thrusts into its research and policy agenda to accelerate gender mainstreaming in infrastructure and align with SDG 5:

(i)   incorporate a gender perspective into data collection practice,
(ii)   extend or complement the OECD framework-specific guidance to incorporate a gender perspective, and
(iii) involve active engagement with the government and private sector to increase women's representation in infrastructure decision-making processes, and the application of OECD Due Diligence Guidance for Responsible Business Conduct.

The OECD and Georgia's Ministry of Economy and Sustainable Development jointly organized a National Policy Dialogue on Improving Access to Green Finance for Small and Medium-Sized Enterprises in Georgia. To accelerate this agenda, there is a need to consider a broad, global partnership. Engagement with the United Nations family, international organizations, multilateral finance institutions, private corporations, and civil society will help accelerate transformations in society and economic processes and deliver on the SDGs in Georgia.

A City Safe for Women

Inclusive urban planning should create environments that are safe and accessible for women. Cities that are safe for women are important in realizing gender equality, social participation, and the protection of women's rights. Planning for gender-sensitive infrastructure is closely linked to the safety and security of public spaces, and residential and recreational areas. Inadequate planning and design can increase the risk of violence, leading to gender isolation and discrimination, as uncontrolled urbanization is linked to increasing risks for women. Various agencies are responsible for creating an urban environment that is safe from violence against women. To realize gender-inclusive cities, it is essential that women participate in governance. In 2015, only 11% of the members of Parliament in Georgia were women.[28]

The World Bank's *Handbook for Gender-Inclusive Urban Planning Design* defines the following factors as inequalities in the built environment for women:

- Women struggle to access opportunities for prosperity such as education and employment.
- Women struggle to be financially independent and accumulate wealth.
- Women's expenses on basic services are higher.

---

[28] Asian Development Bank. 2019. *Future Cities, Future Women Initiative: Phase 1.* Final Report. Manila.

- Women have less freedom, limiting their social and support networks.
- Women experience barriers to participating in decision-making, such as shaping the built environment.[29]

According to the handbook, gender equity in the built environment can "unlock more inclusive economic and social development," suggesting that there are opportunities for inclusive design of the built environment.

A city that is safe for women is one where

- women and girls can safely use public spaces and public transport;
- there is no violence against women in the streets, public gardens, homes, and other areas;
- women and girls are not victims of discrimination and are fully involved in political, cultural, and social life; and
- women are economically independent.

Figure 3 highlights some of the components of cities that are safe for women. Consideration of these aspects ensures the active involvement of women in social life. This will also help prevent violence and discrimination, especially against the most vulnerable female population, such as women with disabilities, single mothers, mothers with many children, elderly women, and girls. A survey conducted under ADB's work on gender inclusion in Georgia shows that 45% of female respondents had experienced sexual harassment in public transport in the previous 6 months (footnote 29).

Travel patterns vary by gender. Women travel less often and in shorter distances than men. Well-developed public transport services, especially buses and trains, can improve their mobility and access to public transport. However, the safety and security of these modes of transport is another important issue determining women's mobility.

A focus on built environment aspects that directly affect the daily life of women, such as safety of public spaces and transport and good lighting, should be considered and can be facilitated through gender-inclusive planning approach. Women's access to social life can be limited due to the barriers they experience in the built environment. Women's safety, access to public transport, and communication networks and services must be improved. This is important not only for their active involvement in social life and access to knowledge, but also to give them access to better employment opportunities.

Decentralizing cities, or considering neighborhoods, is one of the approaches that could help create a more inclusive environment for women. Increased proximity to different daily life activities is beneficial for everyone, including children, the elderly, and PWDs, creating a more inclusive and accessible built environment. One of the main ideas of the concept 'city of short distances' is for individuals to be able to perform everyday tasks easily and independently through providing a unified environment for work, family life, shopping, and accessing services.[30]

---

[29]   World Bank and Kounkuey Design Initiative. 2020. *Handbook for Gender-Inclusive Urban Planning Design*. Washington, DC.
[30]   Urban Development. 2013. *Manual for Gender Mainstreaming in Urban Planning and Urban Development*. Vienna. https://www.wien.gv.at/stadtentwicklung/studien/pdf/b008358.pdf.

Figure 3: Urban Planning Considerations to Ensure a City Safe for Women

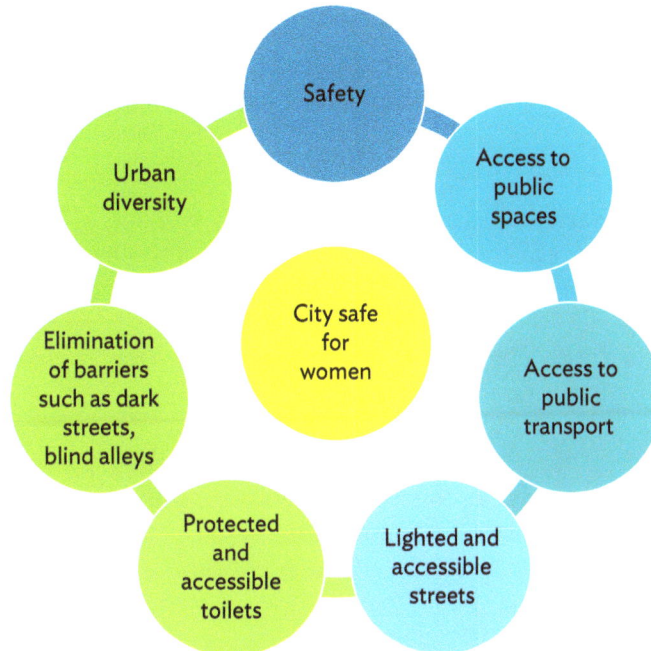

Source: United Nations Entity for Gender Equality and the Empowerment of Women (UN Women). 2011. *Building Safe and Inclusive Cities for Woman: A Practical Guide.* New Delhi.

To develop inclusive neighborhoods, the daily life requirements of different user groups should be reflected in the design of buildings and public spaces. The needs of different groups should, therefore, be evaluated and considered in the planning and design of all projects. The World Bank suggests the following principles for gender-inclusive planning:[31]

- **Participatory.** Actively including the voices of women, girls, and sexual and gender minorities.
- **Integrated.** Adopting a holistic, crosscutting approach that centers gender throughout and promotes citizen-city relationship building.
- **Universal.** Meeting the needs of women, girls, and sexual and gender minorities of all ages and abilities.
- **Knowledge building.** Seeking out and sharing robust, meaningful new data on gender equity.
- **Power building.** Growing the capacity and influence of underrepresented groups in key decisions.
- **Invested in** committing the necessary finances and expertise to follow through on intentional gender equity goals.

---

[31]   World Bank and Kounkuey Design Initiative. 2020. *Handbook for Gender-Inclusive Urban Planning Design.* Washington, DC.

In Georgia, the development of the "Fair Shared City Guidelines" identifies optimal density and arrangement of residential areas, mobility, safety and security, and social infrastructure as key areas of urban design and planning.[32] The successful inclusive development of these areas of city planning can be enhanced through a universal design approach that considers aspects of not only gender-inclusive design, but design that is reflective of diversity and all social groups that may be excluded from the built environment.

Child-Friendly Cities

An inclusive built environment should also consider the needs of children. Creativity and curiosity are the central developmental aspect of children. Children need environments for physical development that include play and learning. The physical environment is one of the factors that influences and supports children's learning. How the physical environment, including buildings, interiors, and outdoor spaces, is designed impacts a child's behavior. Children perceive the environment differently than adults and they typically use and interact with it more.

Designing for children must be based on the principle of the uniqueness of each child, particularly children with disabilities. Designing for all children means creating an environment that is usable by all children without the need for adaptation. That environment must also be free from physical, social, and attitudinal barriers. The creation of such an environment cannot be the responsibility of only one agency responsible for urban planning or architecture. It requires joint efforts of various government, nongovernment, business, and civil society players.

In all actions concerning children, whether undertaken by public or private social welfare institutions, courts of law, administrative authorities, or legislative bodies, the best interests of the child must be the primary consideration. The International Secretariat of the Child Friendly Cities Initiative lays out the nine principles for local administrations to create a child-friendly environment:

(i)   children's participation at all stages of planning and implementation,
(ii)   child-friendly legislation,
(iii)   a child rights strategy,
(iv)   a coordinating agency for children,
(v)   assessment of the impact of policies and programs on children,
(vi)   a budget and resources for children,
(vii)   regular reporting,
(viii) awareness raising and capacity building on child rights, and
(ix)   independent advocacy for children.

The child-friendly cities approach varies according to the level of country development. For example, most high-income countries can afford to focus on urban planning, a safe and green environment, and child participation. However, many low-income countries prioritize social services delivery, health, nutrition, education, and child protection.

---

[32]   Asian Development Bank. 2019. *Future Cities, Future Women Initiative: Phase 1.* Final Report. Manila.

It is challenging for any city administration to target the creation of child-friendly environment and design in the city. Child-friendly design is an integral part of universal design as it should cover the needs and interests of all groups of the population. One of the focuses of universal design is ensuring a child-friendly environment based on the implementation of child rights in accordance with the United Nations Convention on the Rights of the Child.

Child-friendly universal design covers four key aspects:

- **Equitable use.** Designing for all children means creating spaces that are free from social barriers. Indoor and outdoor spaces must allow for positive interpersonal interaction and socialization between children of different abilities and genders. Spaces must be available for small groups, solitude, quiet play, large groups, and active play. Appropriate space will create opportunities for developing self-confidence and social skills.
- **Flexibility and independence.** Designing for all children means understanding that children vary in size, and sometimes this is not directly related to chronological age. It is essential to use a variety of anthropometric charts that can be adjusted based on children's motor skills, and to recognize that many children with disabilities do not follow typical growth patterns.
- **Safety.** Creating designs for all children requires adherence to various mandatory and voluntary safety guidelines for both children and staff. The design should support active experimentation and risk-taking without being unsafe by arranging the physical environment and equipment in a way that minimizes hazards and errors. Another aspect of safety is related to the risk of sexual harassment and violence that girls and women face in urban public spaces. The risk and reality of violence limit their freedom to exercise their rights to education, work, and recreation. This particularly relates to children living in poverty as they are more exposed to these risks. Children who have access to internet are exposed to additional hazards related to uncontrolled information flow, online exploitation, cyber bullying, and internet addiction.
- **Team effort.** Designing for all children requires a multidisciplinary, cross-functional design team from the outset. The experts who design the facility and those who operate it should meet around the same table to create the design program, goals, and requirements together. Program goals; building use; and the needs of children, staff, and parents drive the concurrent design process. Designing for all children finds a way to support and encourage each child's abilities, similarities, and uniqueness. Participatory decision-making is one of the steps toward creating an inclusive city.[33]

Underpinning child-friendly planning and programming is a human-rights-based approach that considers the principles of equality and non-discrimination. Children are recognized as rights holders who should be involved in the planning and implementation of measures that directly affect them.

In conclusion, applying universal design to a child-friendly city contributes to urban inclusiveness, which is important in reducing inequality and increasing local ownership of development processes and programs.

---

[33] ADB. 2017. *Enabling Inclusive Cities: Tool Kit for Inclusive Urban Development.* Manila; World Bank. Inclusive Cities. https://www.worldbank.org/en/topic/inclusive-cities.

Age-Friendly Cities

Both developed and developing countries are experiencing population aging and urbanization simultaneously. By the year 2050, 2 billion people will be aged 60 or over, an increase from 12% to 22% of the world's population.[34] Planning and design solutions looking to address rapid urbanization should consider how to plan the urban environment along universal design principles to create safe cities for the elderly and promote their full and active involvement in social life. An age-friendly city ensures continued inclusion and equality in the built environment across people's life courses.

The benefits of an age-friendly city relate to a healthy lifestyle. As people get older, they can experience a decline in physical and mental health, particularly from noncommunicable diseases, which can mean they are more reliant on health services and community-based support. The greatest causes of disability in the elderly are

- sensory impairments,
- back and neck pain,
- chronic obstructive pulmonary diseases,
- depressive disorders,
- falls,
- diabetes,
- dementia, and
- osteoarthritis.

The physical environment in which people live also influences their ability to age in good health, suggesting that inclusive urban development could have extensive benefits. An inclusive and age-friendly city can enable the continued participation of the elderly in society and minimize detrimental impacts of the physical environment on people's health throughout their life.

The work of the World Health Organization (WHO) on healthy aging proposes that both people and the environments they inhabit are dynamic and constantly changing. Therefore, it is important to have clear principles for urban planning that account for flexibility and change, and for people's diverse needs and desires.

The age-friendly city concept employs the principles of universal design to ensure accessibility, safety, and inclusion for all in urban design. The process of developing an age-friendly city requires the active cooperation of stakeholders from the public and private sectors and civil society. Government should develop a long-term strategy to ensure the creation of a decent, accessible, and healthy environment for the elderly.

An age-friendly city is an inclusive community environment. WHO defines the eight connected "domains of urban life" for healthy aging:

(i)   community and healthcare,
(ii) transportation,

---

[34]   WHO. 10 Facts on Ageing and the Life Course. https://www.who.int/features/factfiles/ageing/en/.

(iii) housing,

(iv) social participation,

(v) outdoor spaces and buildings,

(vi) respect and social inclusion,

(vii) civic participation and employment, and

(viii) communication and information.[35]

These domains can be used to identify both barriers and opportunity areas for more inclusive urban life. Figure 4 details some of the key indicators that can serve as basis for measuring progress across these domains. Monitoring and evaluation should be an integral part of developing age-friendly policies, programs, infrastructures, or places. The main criteria for evaluating an age-friendly city are

- equality,

- safety,

- accessibility of physical environment, and

- economic sustainability.

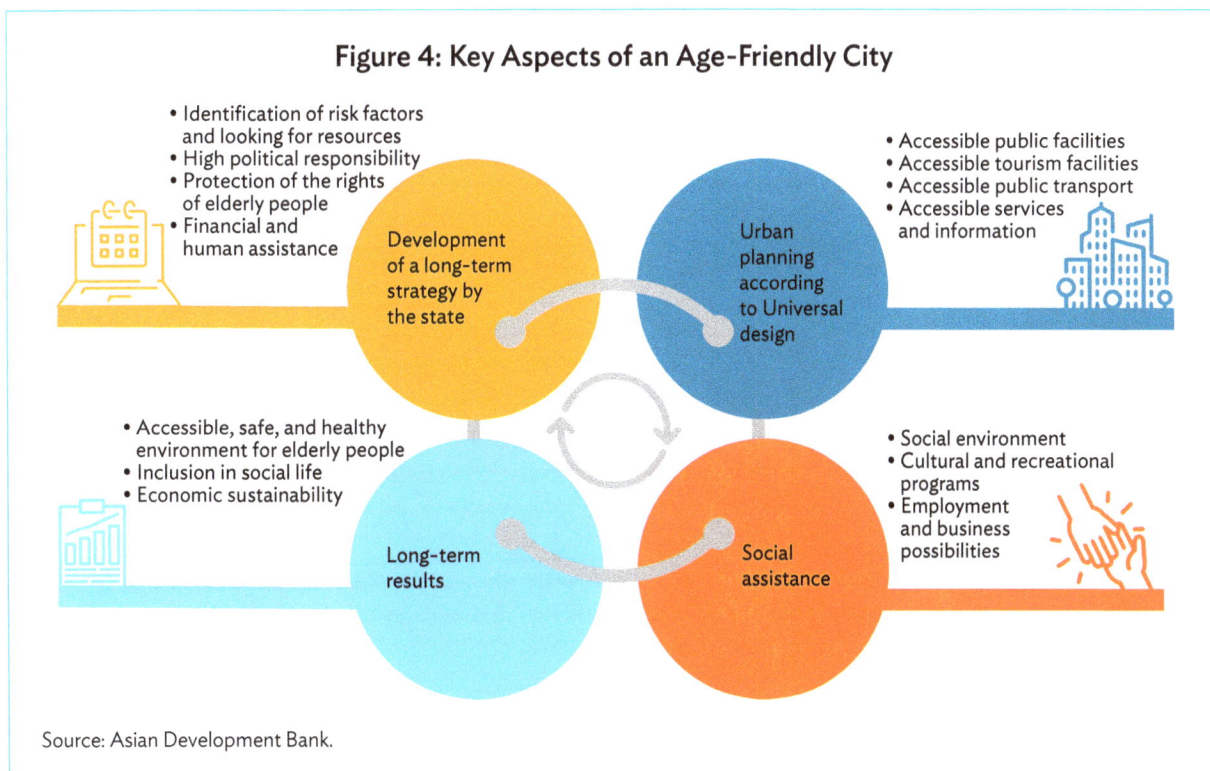

Figure 4: Key Aspects of an Age-Friendly City

- Identification of risk factors and looking for resources
- High political responsibility
- Protection of the rights of elderly people
- Financial and human assistance

Development of a long-term strategy by the state

- Accessible public facilities
- Accessible tourism facilities
- Accessible public transport
- Accessible services and information

Urban planning according to Universal design

- Accessible, safe, and healthy environment for elderly people
- Inclusion in social life
- Economic sustainability

Long-term results

Social assistance

- Social environment
- Cultural and recreational programs
- Employment and business possibilities

Source: Asian Development Bank.

---

35   WHO. 2015. The WHO Age-Friendly Cities Framework. https://extranet.who.int/agefriendlyworld/age-friendly-cities-framework/.

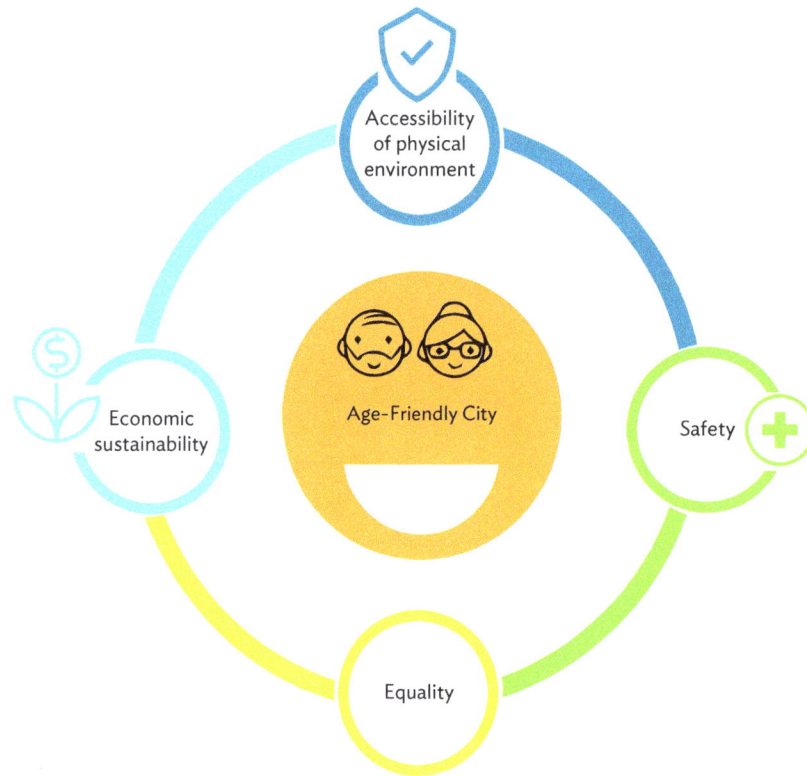

Figure 5: Main Criteria in Evaluating the Age-Friendliness of Cities

Source: World Health Organization. 2015. *Measuring the Age-Friendliness of Cities: A Guide to Using Core Indicators*. Kobe.

An Intersectional Approach

The different aspects of inclusion or exclusion are interrelated and cannot be addressed in isolation. One of the methods to address the complexity of the intersecting challenges associated with achieving inclusive and accessible urban development and tourism is to take an intersectional approach.

Intersectional approaches recognize and adapt to the complexity of identity of individuals and social groups, understanding that gender, disability, race, ethnicity, sexual orientation, and socioeconomic background are all factors that shape an identity.

Intersectional approaches precisely recognize that these factors can be connected, or intersecting, and create inequality in more than one aspect of a person's life.[36] For an inclusive urban development to take place, it is important to recognize how people may experience multiple factors that produce exclusion and inequality, such as being disabled and being female. An intersectional approach can help understand the social, cultural, political, and historical contexts that may be creating exclusion and inaccessibility in the built environment.

---

[36]   D. Chaplin, J. Twigg, and E. Lovell. 2019. Intersectional Approaches to Vulnerability Reduction and Resilience Building: A Scoping Study. *Resilience Intel*. London: BRACED and ODI.

International and National Laws and Regulations

Approaches to inclusive development are guided by both international and national frameworks and legislation (Figure 6).

Figure 6: Visualization of International and National Frameworks and Legislation

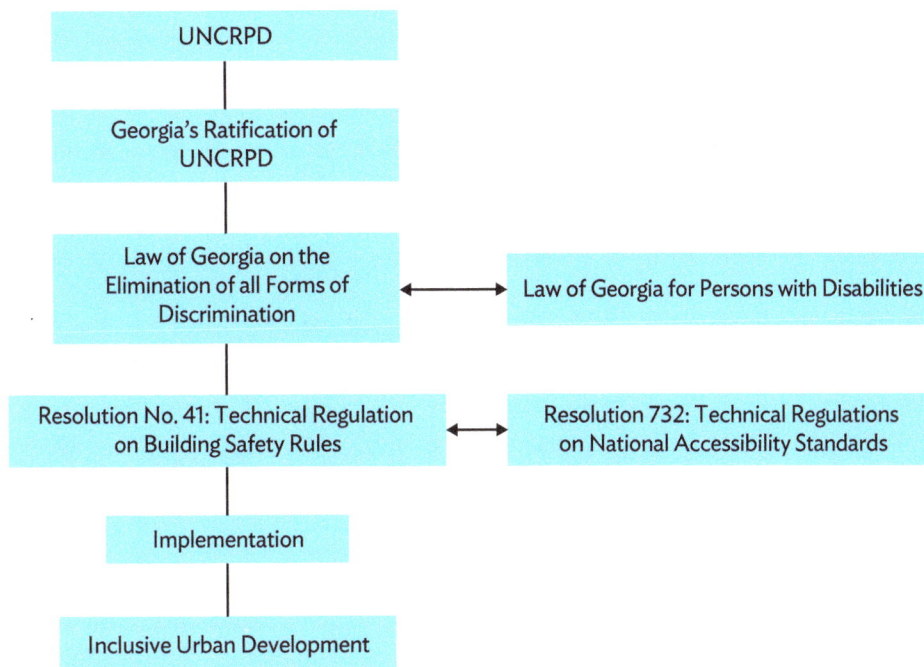

UNCRPD

Georgia's Ratification of UNCRPD

Law of Georgia on the Elimination of all Forms of Discrimination ⟷ Law of Georgia for Persons with Disabilities

Resolution No. 41: Technical Regulation on Building Safety Rules ⟷ Resolution 732: Technical Regulations on National Accessibility Standards

Implementation

Inclusive Urban Development

UNCRPD = United Nations Convention on the Rights of Persons with Disabilities.
Source: Asian Development Bank.

The United Nations Convention on the Rights of Persons with Disabilities

The UNCRPD is an international treaty and the first legally binding instrument with comprehensive protection of the rights of persons with disabilities (PWDs).

The Convention clearly defines the obligations of states to promote, protect, and ensure the rights of PWDs. By signing the Convention, state parties take the responsibility to develop and carry out policies, laws, and administrative measures for securing the rights recognized in the Convention and to abolish laws, regulations, customs, and practices that constitute discrimination (Article 4).[37]

---

[37] United Nations Convention on the Rights of Persons with Disabilities.

Countries should guarantee that persons with disabilities enjoy their inherent right to life on an equal basis with others (Article 10), ensure the equal rights and advancement of women and girls with disabilities (Article 6), and protect children with disabilities (Article 7).[38]

The Convention recognizes the importance of international cooperation and its promotion to support national implementation efforts. An innovation in this regard concerns specific references to actions the international community could take to promote international cooperation, such as

- ensuring that international development programs are inclusive of and accessible to persons with disabilities,
- facilitating and supporting capacity building,
- facilitating cooperation in research and access to scientific and technical knowledge, and
- providing technical and economic assistance as appropriate.

The following eight guiding principles underpin the Convention and each one of its specific articles:

(i)   Respect for inherent dignity, individual autonomy including the freedom to make one's own choices, and independence of persons
(ii)   Non-discrimination
(iii) Full and effective participation and inclusion in society
(iv)   Respect for difference and acceptance of persons with disabilities as part of human diversity and humanity
(v)   Equality of opportunity
(vi)   Accessibility
(vii) Equality between men and women
(viii) Respect for the evolving capacities of children with disabilities and respect for the right of children with disabilities to preserve their identities

Georgia was among the 163 countries that signed the Convention. In 2013, Georgia ratified the Convention, which officially came into force on 12 April 2014 (footnote 38) thereby acknowledging the rights of persons with disabilities and Georgia's commitment to implement measures to ensure non-discrimination.

European Disability Strategy 2010–2020

The European Commission's *European Disability Strategy 2010–2020: A Renewed Commitment to a Barrier-Free Europe* provides a framework for actions that all EU member states have committed to pursue. The Strategy aims to combat discrimination and ensure equal opportunities and conditions for persons with disabilities.[39]

---

[38]   Legislative Herald of Georgia. https://matsne.gov.ge/en/document/view/2334289?publication=0 (in Georgian).
[39]   European Commission. 2010. *Communication from the Commission to the European Parliament, the Council, the European Economic and Social Committee and the Committee of the Regions: European Disability Strategy 2010–2020: A Renewed Commitment to a Barrier-Free Europe.* https://eur-lex.europa.eu/LexUriServ/LexUriServ.do?uri=COM%3A2010%3A0636%3AFIN%3AEN%3APDF.

The Strategy provides the backdrop to several EU and national policies and EU regulations, programs, and other initiatives that have been or will be carried out to serve the overall objectives. The Strategy's main objectives are shown in Figure 7.

The 2010–2020 Strategy will be replaced by the new 2021–2030 Strategy which is yet to be published. Results of the 2010–2020 Strategy evaluation review will serve as basis for policy development.[40]

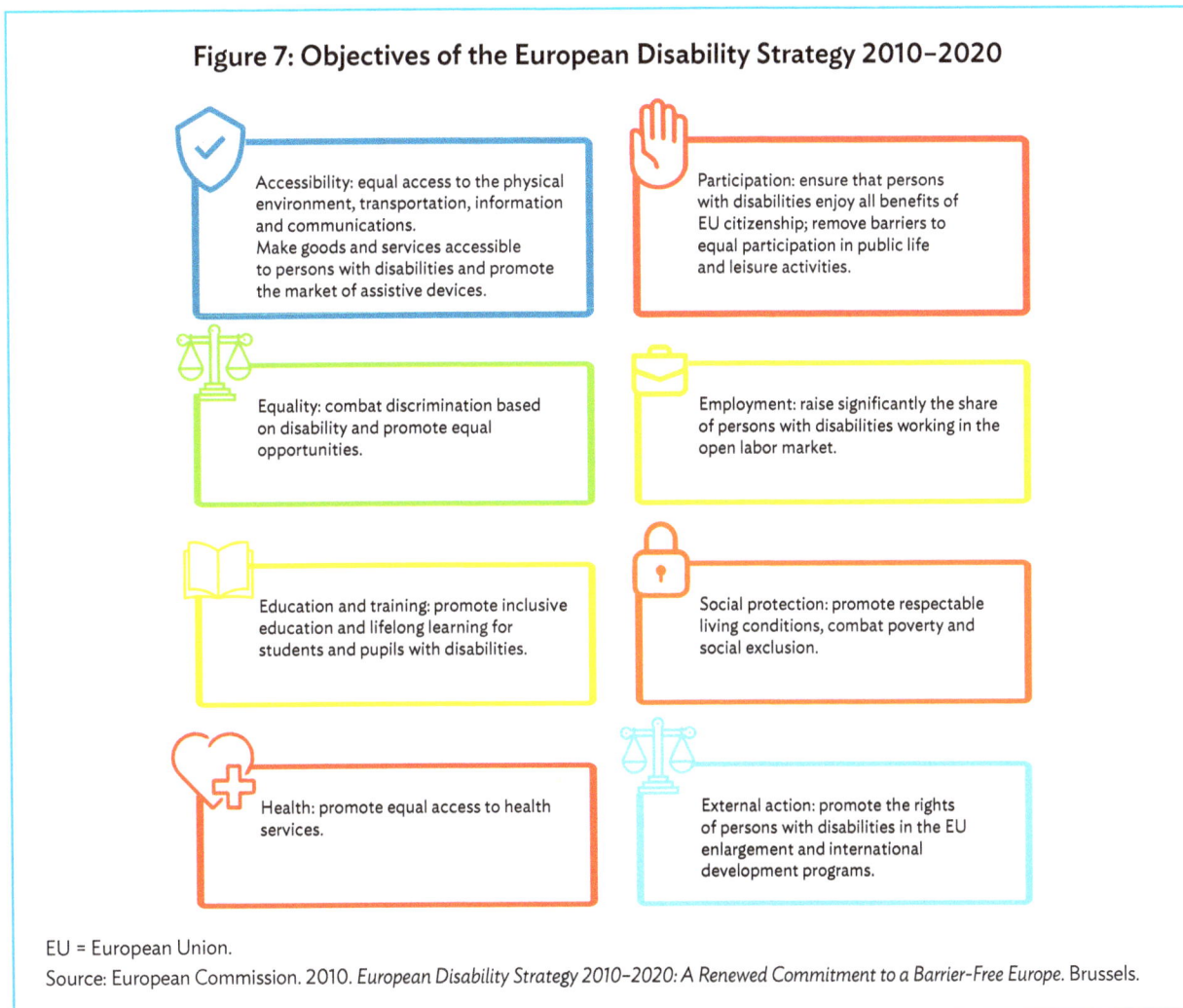

Figure 7: Objectives of the European Disability Strategy 2010–2020

Accessibility: equal access to the physical environment, transportation, information and communications.
Make goods and services accessible to persons with disabilities and promote the market of assistive devices.

Participation: ensure that persons with disabilities enjoy all benefits of EU citizenship; remove barriers to equal participation in public life and leisure activities.

Equality: combat discrimination based on disability and promote equal opportunities.

Employment: raise significantly the share of persons with disabilities working in the open labor market.

Education and training: promote inclusive education and lifelong learning for students and pupils with disabilities.

Social protection: promote respectable living conditions, combat poverty and social exclusion.

Health: promote equal access to health services.

External action: promote the rights of persons with disabilities in the EU enlargement and international development programs.

EU = European Union.
Source: European Commission. 2010. *European Disability Strategy 2010–2020: A Renewed Commitment to a Barrier-Free Europe.* Brussels.

---

[40] European Commission. 2020. *Evaluation of the European Disability Strategy 2010–2020.* https://ec.europa.eu/social/BlobServlet?docId=23191&langId=en.

United Nations World Tourism Organization's Global Code of Ethics and Accessible Tourism

The UN World Tourism Organization's (WTO) Global Code of Ethics 1999 is a comprehensive set of principles designed to guide organizations in tourism development.[41]

Addressed to governments, the travel industry, communities, and tourists, it aims to help maximize the tourism sector's benefits while minimizing its potentially negative impact on the environment, cultural heritage, and societies across the globe. The Code's 10 principles cover the economic, social, cultural, and environmental components of travel and tourism:

Article 1: Tourism's contribution to mutual understanding and respect between peoples and societies

Article 2: Tourism as a vehicle for individual and collective fulfillment

Article 3: Tourism, a factor of sustainable development

Article 4: Tourism, a user of the cultural heritage of mankind and contributor to its enhancement

Article 5: Tourism, a beneficial activity for host countries and communities

Article 6: Obligations of stakeholders in tourism development

Article 7: Right to tourism

Article 8: Liberty of tourist movements

Article 9: Rights of the workers and entrepreneurs in the tourism industry

Article 10: Implementation of the principles of the Global Code of Ethics for Tourism

In 2013, the WTO adopted the updated 2005 document *Accessible Tourism for All*.[42] The 2013 revised manual contains a series of recommendations for the tourism sector that highlight the necessity of providing clear information on the accessibility of tourism facilities, the availability of support services in destinations for persons with disabilities, and the training of employees to build awareness on the diverse needs of persons with disabilities.

Georgian Laws and Regulations

Law of Georgia on the Elimination of all Forms of Discrimination

The purpose of the law is to eliminate every form of discrimination and to ensure equal rights of every natural and legal person under the legislation of Georgia, irrespective of race; skin color; language; sex; age; citizenship; origin; place of birth or residence; property or social status; religion or belief; national, ethnic, or social origin; profession; marital status; health; disability; sexual orientation; gender identity and expression; political or other opinions; or other characteristics.[43]

---

[41]   UN World Tourism Organization. Global Code of Ethics for Tourism. https://www.unwto.org/global-code-of-ethics-for-tourism.

[42]   Resolution A/RES/492(XVI). See http://www.accessibletourism.org/?i=enat.en.news.1476.

[43]   Legislative Herald of Georgia. Law on the Elimination of All Forms of Discrimination. https://matsne.gov.ge/en/document/view/2339687?publication=0.

The Law of Georgia on the Rights of Persons with Disabilities

In 2020, Georgia adopted "the Law of Georgia on the Rights of Persons with Disabilities"[44] which is based on and is applicable according to the Constitution of Georgia, the UN Convention on the Rights of Persons with Disabilities, universally recognized human rights, norms of international law and Georgian legislative normative acts and bylaws. The purpose of the law is to facilitate realization of rights and fundamental freedoms of persons with disabilities. It also provides the basic principles and mechanisms of accessibility for persons with disabilities, without discrimination and on equal basis with others.

The law contains the following important articles on the rights of persons with disabilities: equal recognition before the law (Article 1), independent living (Article 2), non-discrimination (Article 3), women with disabilities (Article 5), children with disabilities (Article 7), education (Article 8), healthcare (Article 9), habilitation and rehabilitation (Article 10), labor and employment (Article 11), protection from exploitation, violence and abuse (Article 12), protection of private and family life (Article 13), participation in political and social life (Article 14), social protection (Article 15), participation in cultural life, sport, leisure and other public events (Article 16), awareness-raising (Article 17), access to legal proceedings (Article 18), and personal assistance (Article 20).

Specifically under Article 21, the Law of Georgia on the Rights of Persons with Disabilities requires the following obligations:

(i)   ensure the introduction of the universal design of existing buildings and buildings under construction, and other types of infrastructure, and/or the adaptation thereof in accordance with universal design for persons with disabilities, in order to ensure full access to all institutions under its governance.

(ii)   ensure full access to all relevant services in its system for persons with disabilities, including offering programs and materials customized and adapted to relevant needs (such as audio books, books printed in Braille, sign language interpretation, subtitles).

(iii)   develop and approve an action plan to ensure adaptation and universal design, for the fulfilment of the obligations determined by sub-paragraphs (a) and (b) of this paragraph, with an indication of measures to be taken and relevant deadlines, as well as provide supervision over their implementation.

(iv)   promote, within its competence, the implementation of a unified strategy and action plan approved by the Government of Georgia.

(v)   ensure the continuous retraining of corresponding personnel for the development of the skills which are required for communicating with persons with disabilities.

(vi)   participate, within its competence, in the development of normative acts, strategies, action plans and instructions provided for by this Law, and facilitate the implementation thereof.

---

44   Government of Georgia. 2020. *"The Law of Georgia on the Rights of Persons with Disabilities"* Tbilisi

Georgia Tourism Strategy 2015–2025

In agreement with the Ministry of Economy and Sustainable Development of Georgia and with financing from the World Bank, the Georgian National Tourism Administration developed the Georgia Tourism Strategy 2015–2025.[45] This document aims to enhance the role of tourism in developing the country's economy and to improve the living conditions of the population. Its eight strategic objectives are shown in Figure 8.

Figure 8: Eight Strategic Objectives of the Georgia Tourism Strategy 2015–2025

Respect, enhance, and protect Georgia's natural and cultural heritage

Create unique and authentic visitor experiences, centered on those natural and cultural assets

Enhance competitiveness through delivery of excellent visitor service

Attract higher market spending through increased and more effective marketing and promotion

Expand and enhance Georgia's ability to collect and analyze tourism data and measure industry performance

Enhance the business environment to facilitate increased foreign and domestic investment

Expand public and private sector investment in the tourism sector

Build partnerships between government industry, nongovernment organizations, and communities that will be needed to achieve all of the above

Source: Georgian National Tourism Administration, Ministry of Economy and Sustainable Development. 2015. *Georgia Tourism Strategy 2025*. Tbilisi.

---

[45]   Ministry of Economy and Sustainable Development of Georgia and Georgian National Tourism Administration. 2015. *Georgian Tourism Strategy 2025* (in Georgian).

Resolution No. 41: Technical Regulations for the Safety Rules for Buildings

In January 2016, the Government of Georgia adopted Resolution No. 41 on Approving Technical Regulations for the Safety Rules for Buildings.[46] This technical rule regulates the planning, fire safety, provision of exit facilities, and other requirements for the design, construction, and use of buildings.

The technical rule covers issues including the accessibility of routes, entrances, living and bedroom units, other means and devices, and the accessibility system of signs. Chapter 11, *Accessbility, Resolution No. 41, Technical Regulation of Building Safety Rules*, indicates that the planning and construction of a building must comply with accessibility rules and Resolution 732 on Technical Regulation: National Accessbility Standards. The chapter headings are shown in Figure 9.[47]

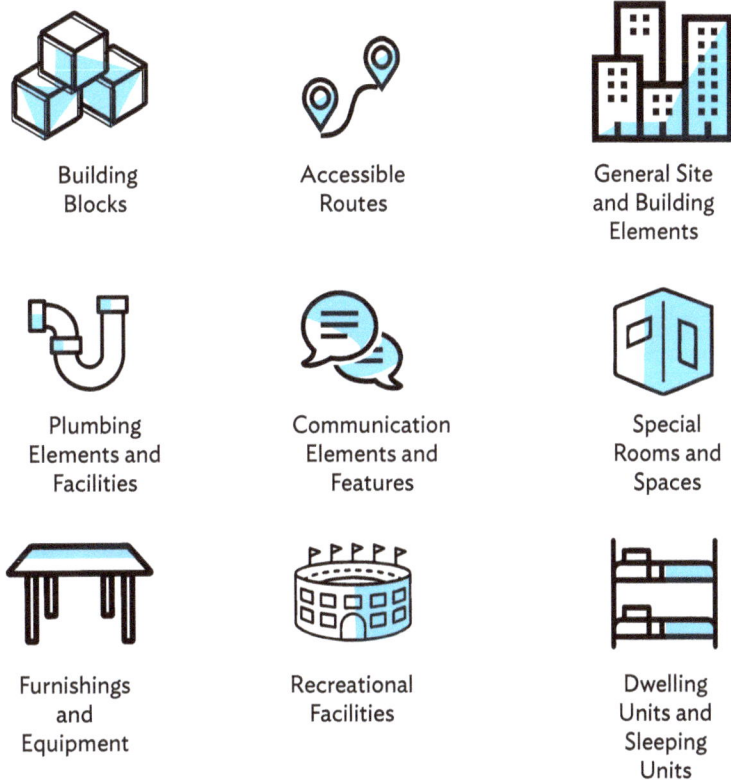

Figure 9: Chapter Headings from Resolution 732 on Technical Regulation: National Accessbility Standards

Building Blocks

Accessible Routes

General Site and Building Elements

Plumbing Elements and Facilities

Communication Elements and Features

Special Rooms and Spaces

Furnishings and Equipment

Recreational Facilities

Dwelling Units and Sleeping Units

Source: Government of Georgia, 2020. Resolution 732 on Technical Resolution: National Accessibility Standards. Tbilisi.

46   Government of Georgia. 2016. Resolution No. 41. Technical Regulation of Building Safety Rules. Tbilisi.
47   Government of Georgia, 2020. Resolution 732 on Technical Resolution: National Accessibility Standards. Tbilisi.

Universal Design and Accessible Tourism Development

Universal Design

Universal Design History

In 1950 in the United States (US), the barrier-free movement started a process of change in public policies to create equal opportunities in areas such as education, employment, and the physical environment for persons with disabilities (PWDs).

The first nationally recognized accessibility standard, A117.1 Accessible and Usable Buildings and Facilities, was published in 1961 by the American National Standards Institute.[48] The concept of universal design grew from the priorities of human-centered design and social goals of civil rights movements throughout the 1960s and 1970s.[49] These ideas included affordable housing, urban revitalization, mental health, aging, and early childhood education.[50]

The Civil Rights Movement also influenced legislation in the 1970s, 1980s, and 1990s. New laws provided access to education, transportation, public accommodation, and telecommunications, and prohibited discrimination against PWDs.

The US federal legislation passed in the late 1960s includes the following:

- The Architectural Barriers Act of 1968
- Section 505 of the Rehabilitation Act of 1973, issued in 1977
- The Education for Handicapped Children Act of 1975
- The Fair Housing Amendments Act of 1988
- The Americans with Disabilities Act of 1990
- The Telecommunications Act of 1996

Ronald L. Mace (1941–1998), American architect, product designer, educator, and creator of the term "universal design," influenced international thinking about design. His architectural and product designs and books are a legacy that continues to influence the world today. A wheelchair user for most of his life, in 1992 he received the President's Award for Distinguished Federal Civilian Service for promoting the dignity, equality, independence, and employment of PWDs. The impact of his work will be felt for generations to come.

---

[48]   American National Standards Institute. 1961. A117.1 *Accessible and Usable Buildings and Facilities*. New York.
[49]   Universal design is the design and composition of an environment so that it can be accessed, understood, and used to the greatest extent possible by all people, regardless of their age, size, ability, or disability. National Disability Authority. What is Universal Design? http://universaldesign.ie/What-is-Universal-Design/.
[50]   E. Steinfeld and J. Maisel. 2012. *Universal Design: Creating Inclusive Environments*. Columbia.

Figure 10 highlights the seven principles of universal design.

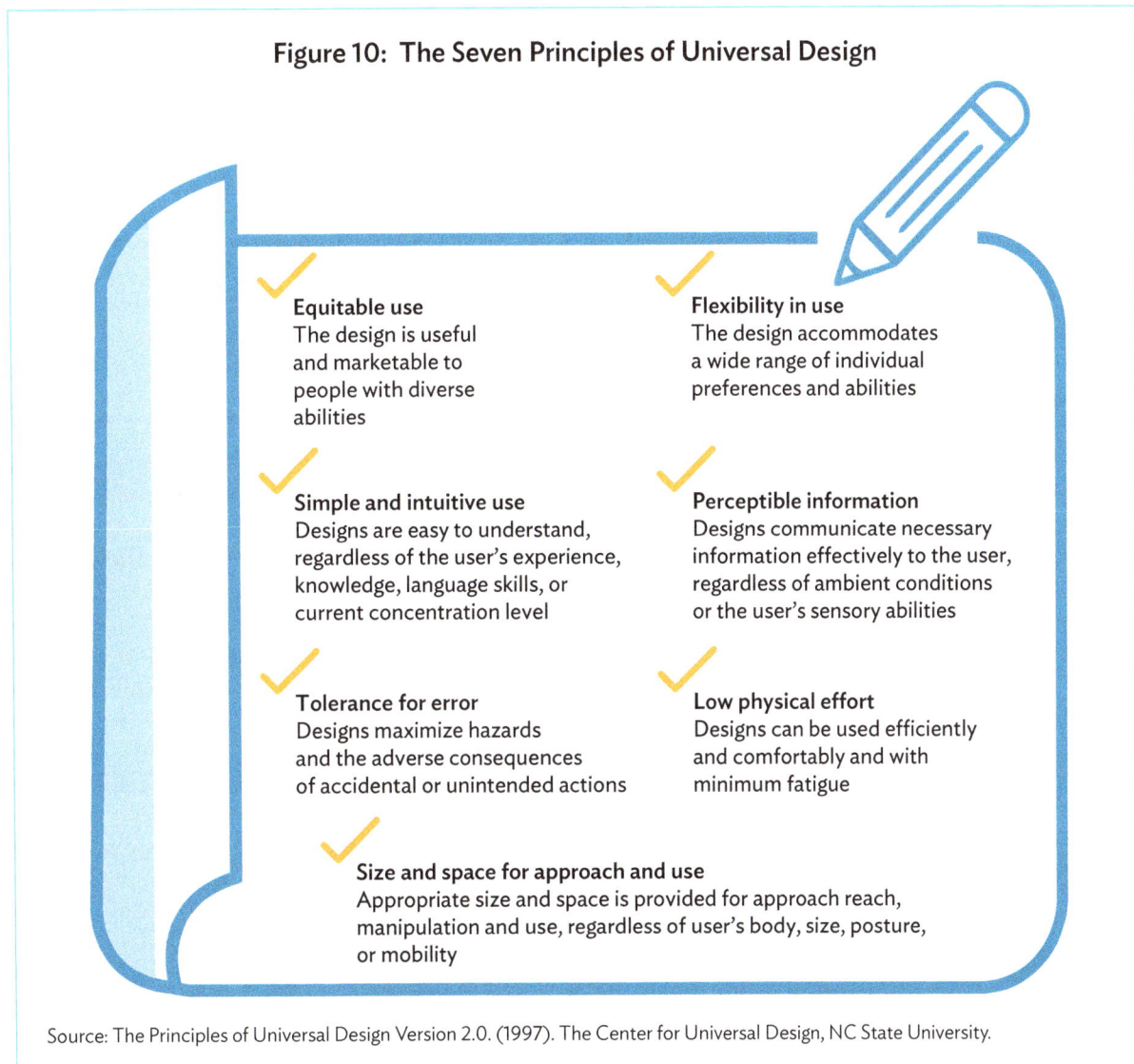

Figure 10: The Seven Principles of Universal Design

✓ **Equitable use**
The design is useful and marketable to people with diverse abilities

✓ **Flexibility in use**
The design accommodates a wide range of individual preferences and abilities

✓ **Simple and intuitive use**
Designs are easy to understand, regardless of the user's experience, knowledge, language skills, or current concentration level

✓ **Perceptible information**
Designs communicate necessary information effectively to the user, regardless of ambient conditions or the user's sensory abilities

✓ **Tolerance for error**
Designs maximize hazards and the adverse consequences of accidental or unintended actions

✓ **Low physical effort**
Designs can be used efficiently and comfortably and with minimum fatigue

✓ **Size and space for approach and use**
Appropriate size and space is provided for approach reach, manipulation and use, regardless of user's body, size, posture, or mobility

Source: The Principles of Universal Design Version 2.0. (1997). The Center for Universal Design, NC State University.

"Universal design is a framework for the design of places, things, information, communication and policy to be usable by the widest range of people operating in the widest range of situations without special or separate design. Most simply, Universal Design is human-centered design of everything with everyone in mind."

The Institute for Human Centered Design

"Universal design is the design of products and environments that is usable by all people, to the greatest extent possible, without the need for adaptation or specialized design."

Ron Mace, 1985

Universal Design in Global Contexts

While universal design has its origins in the US, the principles of universal design and other similar approaches have adopted globally, such as "Inclusive Design" in the United Kingdom (UK) and "Design for All" in Europe.

According to Clarkson and Coleman, what these different approaches have in common is a shift to more inclusive thinking about "us."[51] This shift in design thinking mirrors the shift away from the medical model of disability to the social model of disability, where people are either enabled or disabled by the environment they inhabit, the services they access, and the products they use.

While universal design and design for all can be considered more "aspirational" in their approaches, inclusive design is unique in framing "design exclusion," understanding that people are unique, and that one-size-fits-all solutions do not exist (footnote 52). These approaches now have global reach as recognized through organizations such as the European Institute for Design and Disability (now known as EIDD Design for All Europe), which was established in 1993, and the European Design for Ageing Network (DAN), established in 1994. In 2003, an International Association for Universal Design (IAUD) was established in Japan, and in 2005, the Design for All Institute of India was established.

The *World Report on Disability* highlights how standards for accessible physical environment should take into account local context and culture, which also applies to adopting universal design principles. While these principles are general, every country has specific challenges with respect to inclusive development that should be considered in developing their own inclusive urban development frameworks. An example of this is seen in Japan, where the concept of universal design was adopted from the US, but adapted to the local context. Japan, being a country with a great aging population, specifically focuses on consultation with the elderly and women and children to create an "inclusive communities" approach.

Inclusive urban design should adapt to a country's socioeconomic status, demographics and culture, and geography and climate. In the case of Georgia, the country's mountainous topography will require particular consideration when planning for an inclusive built environment. Factors such as these can make infrastructure development more complex, making it even more imperative that universal design principles are integrated from the start.

Universal Design and Built Heritage

Applying universal design to existing buildings can be more difficult and expensive than for new building development. These challenges can be exacerbated in cultural heritage sites where demands of access may conflict with regulations on conservation and preservation. In a series of recommendations on improving access to historic buildings and places, the National Disability Authority in Ireland proposes the following guidance for applying universal design in places of built heritage:

- Pre-visit information available in accessible formats and providing information about the accessibility of the site and services in advance

---

[51]   P. John Clarkson and R. Coleman. 2013. History of Inclusive Design in the UK. *Applied Ergonomics.* https://doi.org/10.1016/j.apergo.2013.03.002.

- All staff suitably trained in disability and equality awareness
- An accessible external landscape
- Simple and intuitive wayfinding and orientation
- Well-designed and legible signage
- An accessible principal entry point
- Access for everyone to facilities or, where this is not possible, alternative access provided
- Interpretive information available in a variety of formats
- Programs and events that are accessible to all
- Emergency evacuation for everyone[52]

The key principle here is that visitors gain equitable and positive experiences from their visit to a heritage site, regardless of the historic physical restrictions that may be in place. Therefore, this places more emphasis on the delivery of information and services and staff support and attitudes.

Accessible Tourism

Accessible tourism builds links between different actors in the tourism industry, forms partnerships with private actors, stimulates the local economy, and promotes the integration of persons with disabilities and active involvement of local communities. It emphasizes sustainability and accounts for influencing environmental, social, and economic factors.

Key policy instruments and references include

- Human Rights and the United Nations Convention on the Rights of Persons with Disabilities,
- World Health Organization World Report on Disability 2011, [53]
- WTO Tourism Ethics,[54] and
- European Disability Strategy 2010–2020.

The problem of access to tourist facilities for PWDs is now recognized as an issue of global concern by the WTO, governments, tourism authorities, and increasingly by destinations, tourism operators, and nongovernment organizations.

The need to take action to improve accessibility as a dimension of tourism provision has been highlighted since 1990, which was declared the European Year of Tourism. At the Tourism for All in Europe Conference held that year, it was stated "Direct interface between tourism organisations and representatives of disabled people's groups will be a major step forward in this area, shifting emphasis

---

[52] Government of Ireland, National Disability Authority. 2011. *Access: Improving the Accessibility of Historic Building and Places.* Dublin. p. 16. http://nda.ie/Publications/Environment-Housing/Environment-Publications/Access-Improving-the-accessibility-of-historic-buildings-and-places.html.

[53] World Health Organization and World Bank. 2011. *World Report on Disability.* https://www.who.int/disabilities/world_report/2011/report.pdf.

[54] WTO. 1999. *Tourism Ethics.* https://www.unwto.org/global-code-of-ethics-for-tourism?fbclid=IwAR0rgxeZvmI-Um2OUAOMXtUhiELdwyNvLFt8p_zJtZJ91m6ZXd5JhgThXfs.

from "social needs provision" and allowing persons with disabilities (and their families) to enjoy the same access as able-bodied people to a full range of tourism resources."[55]

Remarkably, the development of accessible tourism began even earlier. The late 1980s saw the emergence in the UK of a movement named "Tourism for All." The Baker Report, published in 1989, triggered the movement.[56] The report recommends that the United Kingdom's tourism industry should make its services accessible to all customers, regardless of their ability or disability, age, family, or financial situation.

Several other European organizations subsequently began to focus on these and on similar issues. Soon, the Tourism for All campaign was taken up and developed in several other countries under names such as Tourisme Pour Tous (France), Tourismus für Alle (Germany), Turismo per Tutti (Italy), and Turism för Alla (Sweden).

The common denominator and the philosophy of this concept was quality. The demands for quality and comfort are not contradictory to accessibility. Indeed, accessibility is a prerequisite for comfort, safety, and inclusion. Inclusive design, therefore, is a good design.

To create a good product, environment, or service that can be used equitably by all people, the needs of a broad range of potential users must be considered. The Nordic Council of Ministers set this objective in their 2002 Declaration, "Everyone should be able to travel to the country, within the country and to whatever place, attraction or event they should wish to visit."[57]

The EU named 2003 as the European Year of People with Disabilities with many successful campaigns and events held all over Europe. Anna Diamantopoulou, a member of the European Commission in charge of employment and social affairs, set up an expert group with the mandate to prepare a report on how to address accessibility within an increasingly diverse and aging society.[58]

The first EU Disability Action Plan 2003–2010 recognizes that each sector of the government should establish policies and actions to address accessibility for PWDs. This led to numerous actions at the EU and national levels wherein "sector responsibility for accessibility" was widely adopted. In the tourism sector, achieving Tourism for All depends on the integration of a number of policy elements in several policy areas, including industrial, regional, and national development policies as well as disability and employment

> *"Direct interface between tourism organisations and representatives of disabled people's groups will be a major step forward in this area, shifting emphasis from 'social needs provision' and allowing persons with disabilities (and their families) to enjoy the same access as able-bodied people to a full range of tourism resources"*
>
> Toerisme Vlaanderen, 2001

---

[55] ENAT. 2007. *Towards 2010: Disability Policy Challenges and Actions for the European Tourism Sector.* https://www.accessibletourism.org/resources/enat_study_3_policy_en-2.pdf.

[56] M. Baker. 1989. *Tourism for All: A Report of the Working Party Chaired by Mary Baker.* London: English Tourist Board (in association with the Holiday Care Service, the Scottish Tourist Board, and the Wales Tourist Board).

[57] Nordic Council of Ministers 2002 Declaration. https://sustainabledevelopment.un.org/index.php?page=view&type=255&nr=19745.

[58] European Commission. 2003. 2010: A Europe Accessible For All. http://www.accessibletourismorg/?i=enat.en.reports.442.

policies. Environment, transport, information and communication technology, and education policies (related to the training of architects and planners in universal design) could also be added.

In 2014, the EU commissioned three large-scale mapping studies related to accessible tourism. The studies focus on

(i)   skills requirements in accessible tourism;
(ii)   market demand and economic impact of accessible tourism, with projections to 2020; and
(iii)   mapping the supply and checking the performance of accessible tourism services in Europe.

These studies demonstrated the need for new training programs to meet the needs of tourists with access requirements. In addition, the results of market studies at the national and international levels clearly indicate the size of the potential market and economic significance represented by persons with disabilities and older visitors (Figure 12). Each study also produced case studies identifying good practices in skills and training, accessible tourism business development, and accessible tourism destinations. These are available on the European Network for Accessible Tourism (ENAT) website.[59]

The United Nations Economic and Social Commission for Asia and the Pacific (UNESCAP) Takayama Declaration (2009) defines accessible tourism as "catering to the needs of a full range of consumers including persons with disabilities, older persons and cross-generational families. It entails removal of attitudinal and institutional barriers in society, and encompasses accessibility in the physical environment, in transportation, information and communications and other facilities and services. It encompasses publicly and privately-owned tourist locations."[60]

Persons with disabilities and the elderly are a significant segment of the tourism market, and their travel frequency could be increased if the conditions for safe and accessible tourism were fulfilled. If the demand is met satisfactorily, the economic return and employment rate could be improved by their additional spending. Tourism operators are, therefore, incentivized to implement business strategies with these market segments in mind and with a view toward the long-term demographic changes in the market.

Customer care is one factor that needs to be considered. Satisfying a customer with specific needs requires an understanding of the nature of those needs to respond appropriately to requests and prepare an adequate product or service. Another very important factor is to be able to offer an integrated tourist product chain in which all elements meet the needs and demands of tourists with disabilities, and a service supply chain that can be enjoyed as a whole and in its individual elements.

"Accessible tourism refers to tourism that caters to the needs of a full range of consumers including persons with disabilities, older persons and cross-generational families. It entails removal of attitudinal and institutional barriers in society, and encompasses accessibility in the physical environment, in transportation, information and communications and other facilities and services. It encompasses publicly and privately-owned tourist locations."

UN Asia-Pacific Regional Forum

59   ENAT. 2014. *Proceedings of the European Conference: Mind the Accessibility Gap.* Brussels. https://www.accessibletourism. org/?i=enat.en.presentations.1578.
60   UN-ESCAP. 2009. Congress on the Creation of an Inclusive and Accessible Community in Asia and the Pacific; UN. 2009. *UN Asia-Pacific Regional Forum Recommends Ways to Promote Accessibility for Persons with Disabilities.* https://www.accessibletourism. org/?i=enat.en.news.719.

Market Size and Economic Benefit

Accessible tourism is a rapidly growing segment of the world travel industry. The World Health Organization estimates that 1 billion people (15% of the world's population) live with some form of disability. Figure 11 shows the estimated number of PWDs in the EU, the People's Republic of China, and the US.

Figure 11: Persons with Disabilities in the European Union, the People's Republic of China, and the United States

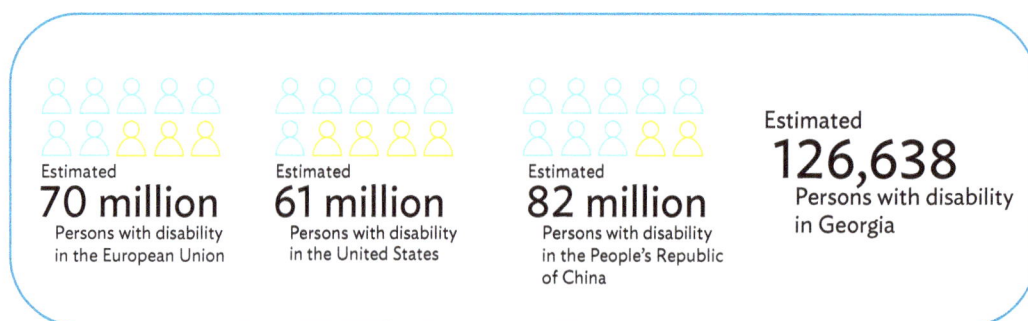

Estimated
70 million
Persons with disability
in the European Union

Estimated
61 million
Persons with disability
in the United States

Estimated
82 million
Persons with disability
in the People's Republic
of China

Estimated
126,638
Persons with disability
in Georgia

Source: European Commission. 2019. Disability Statistics. https://ec.europa.eu/eurostat/statistics-explained/index.php?title=Disability_statistics; Centers for Disease Control and Prevention. 2019. Disability Impacts All of Us. https://www.cdc.gov/ncbddd/disabilityandhealth/infographic-disability-impacts-all.html; China Disabled Persons' Federation. http://www.cdpf.org.cn/english/index.shtml.

The European Commission's final report, *Economic Impact and Travel Patterns of Accessible Tourism in Europe 2014,* states that travelers within the EU who required special access, whether due to disability or age, undertook 783 million trips within the region, contributing €394 billion to the EU economy and creating 8.7 million jobs. The report named France, Germany, Italy, and the UK as the major European source markets for EU's accessible tourism.

Accessible tourism benefits everyone. It is not only about persons with disabilities. It can also benefit the people accompanying them, as well as the elderly, families traveling with children, and people with temporary disabilities. The European study found that two-thirds of the visitors with access needs were the elderly (aged 65 plus) and one-third were PWDs. However, it did not count the large numbers of families with young children, who also have significant access requirements when traveling because of stroller and pushchair use and large amounts of luggage.

National visitor surveys in 2009 by Visit Britain, the official tourism website of the UK, showed that overnight trips made or accompanied by a person with an impairment accounted for 5.7 million trips within a 6-month period and contributed about £1 billion to the UK domestic visitor economy.[61] Trips by visitors who have specific access needs accounted for about 12% of all trips.

---

[61]   VisitBritain VisitEngland. GB Tourism Survey: archive. https://www.visitbritain.org/archive-great-britain-tourism-survey-overnight-data.

The 2013 UK visitor survey research on trips by groups where a member of the party has an impairment reveals the following figures:

- Total day trips: 271 million, with a total spend of £9.4 billion
- Total domestic overnight trips: 14 million, with a total spend of £2.7 billion
- Inbound trips: 0.6 million, with a total spend of £0.3 billion
- Total number of trips: 285.6 million
- Total spending: £12.4 billion
- Average length of stay: 3.3 nights against 2.9 for all tourists
- Average spending: £191 against £184 for all tourists
- Increase in visitor numbers since 2009: 19%
- Increase in value since 2009: 33%

These figures confirm that tourists with disabilities or other access needs make up a significant proportion of the total market and that the numbers (and value) of this segment is rising faster than other customer groups.

The tourism sector in Georgia is already showing strong signs of growth (Figure 12). In 2018, there were 8,679,544 international visitor trips, representing an annual growth rate of 9.8% (excluding non-resident citizens of Georgia). In 2017, the annual growth rate was 17.6%.[62]

Figure 12: Georgia International Traveler Trips, 2016–2018

2016 — 6,719,975

2017 — 7,902,509

2018 — 8,679,544

Source: National Statistics Office of Georgia and Georgia National Tourism Administration. https://gnta.ge/statistics/.

---

[62]   National Statistics Office of Georgia and Georgia National Tourism Administration. https://gnta.ge/statistics/.

Accessible Tourism Development

For successful development of accessible tourism, several key tools and resources are needed to help leverage and support the public and private sectors and enable them to respond to a call to action at the national, regional, and local levels, and enjoy all the benefits that accessibility can offer them and their customers.

The building blocks (as shown in Figure 13), based on studies by ENAT, indicate the four key areas that need to be addressed to create accessible destinations and tourism businesses.

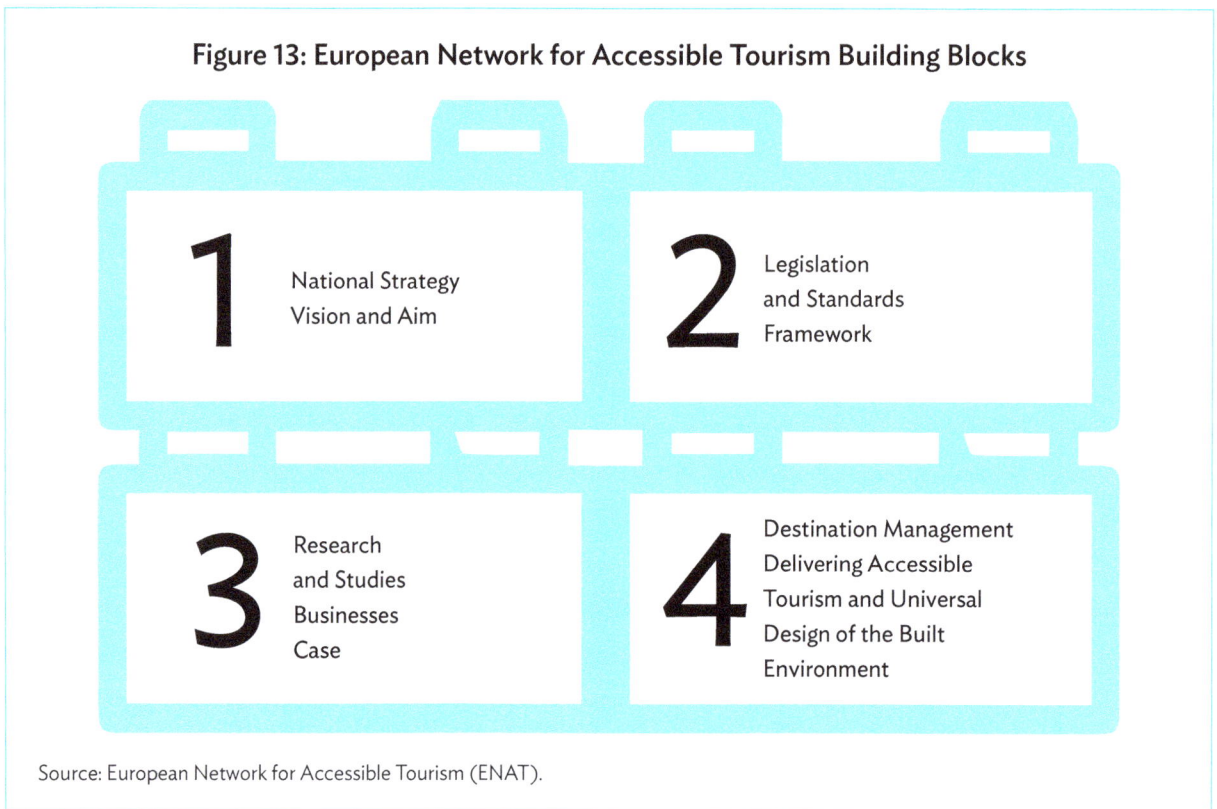

Figure 13: European Network for Accessible Tourism Building Blocks

1 National Strategy Vision and Aim

2 Legislation and Standards Framework

3 Research and Studies Businesses Case

4 Destination Management Delivering Accessible Tourism and Universal Design of the Built Environment

Source: European Network for Accessible Tourism (ENAT).

1. National strategy vision and aim

- Create a local policy for accessibility of the built environment and accessible tourism development, with funding and an action plan for an initial period of 2–3 years, with tangible objectives and measurable goals.
- Set up pilot projects in selected areas that have good preconditions (physical, organizational, and human resources), to establish working groups and develop and test solutions on a small scale.
- Monitor and report on a regular basis, review and adapt the action plan as necessary.
- Identify key actions that can be implemented more widely.
- Implement the plan across the whole of the local area at the end of the pilot phase.

2. **Legislation and standards framework**

- Create a working group (that includes persons with disabilities) to draft or update national accessibility guidelines and/or standards.
- Examine how legislation and standards currently operate and can be implemented and enforced in a specific pilot community, city or region, with three actions:
  - » train building inspectors and city and/or transport planners in the application of the new legislation and/or standards through public procurement and management,
  - » develop and test the new guidelines and standards,
  - » establish a conformity assessment scheme and certification or approval procedure.

3. **Research and studies business case**

- Create programs at technical universities and business and tourism management schools to teach and begin research programs on accessibility.
- Provide education and training in customer welcome and customer care for visitors with particular access requirements.
- Conduct market studies on the volume and value of the accessible tourism market.
- Carry out training and studies on universal design of the built environment, and on product and service design.
- Develop accessible information and communication technologies and systems.
- Establish visiting lectureships and exchanges for staff and researchers of Georgian and international universities and training colleges.
- Hold an annual national or international conference on accessible tourism and universal design.

4. **Developing destination management**

- Research and understand the accessible tourism market and develop the local business case.
- Develop policies and a strategy to implement universal design of the built environment and accessible tourism at national, regional, and local levels.
- Raise tourism business awareness with a focus on access.
- Develop access information provision encouraging businesses to produce access statements that describe their facilities and offers for visitors.
- Undertake destination access audits to determine what they have that facilitates accessibility, and how they can improve.
- Ensure promotion and marketing are inclusive.

Access Audit Methodology

An access audit is a tool for assessing the accessibility of the environment, infrastructure, and services. It covers all the important details for ensuring full inclusion of persons with disabilities by eliminating obstacles and barriers that hinder their full participation. It is an important step in improving accessibility and provides the basis for developing an improvement strategy. It is vital that PWDs are consulted through the audit process and are proactively engaged in the development of subsequent strategies.

An access audit generally includes the elements shown in Figure 14.

Figure 14: Elements of an Access Audit

- Roads and streets
- Routes to entrance
- Internal doors
- Furniture
- Public transport stops and waiting sheds
- Entrances and thresholds
- Accessible toilets
- Lighting
- Recreational areas
- Reception facilities and lobbies
- Signage and wayfinding
- Acoustics

- Landscape and street furniture
- Lifts, stairs, ramps, and other level changes
- Exit and refuge areas
- Heating, ventilation, and air-conditioning
- Arrival and parking
- Internal layout and circulation
- Emergency equipment and procedures
- Service and facilities
- Staff and customer care
- Information provision

Source: Accessible Tourism Center. 2018. *Elements of an Access Audit*. Tbilisi.

An access audit is often best undertaken by applying a "journey" sequence approach, with the auditor placing themselves in the position of end users, including visitors, customers, residents, and employees. Often, when auditing a physical building or site, the audit begins not at the front door, but at the point an individual begins to plan the journey there. When considering public facilities, this typically starts with pre-visit information available, often online, and transport services available to and from the site. Only then does the audit begin to consider the physical site including routes to/from the main entrance and all internal aspects of the building including physical infrastructure and the softer operational and management services available.

Consideration must also be given to responsibilities. Different aspects of an audit may have different responsible parties. It is important this is understood in advance and that subsequent recommendations are positioned to be actioned upon accordingly.

Education, Advocacy, and Public Communication

All stakeholders, including public sector bodies, nongovernment organizations, persons with disabilities, disabled people's organizations, local advocacy groups, business entities, investors, and other specialists of universal design should work together to achieve positive changes in Georgia.

Education

Enhancing the quality of education and raising awareness to expand people's understanding of how universal design benefits all of society is essential.

Disability equality and awareness training is also very important, especially for frontline staff. This is especially important in the tourism industry where service provision is a key aspect. Staff must be confident and feel empowered to properly support visitors and customers with disabilities.

Educating staff and providing training can also help reduce and eliminate many of the stigmas often associated with PWDs. This can be most effective when the training is delivered by PWDs themselves.

Through education and the realization of good, inclusive practice, it is possible to create a culture of inclusion.

The Role of the Media

The media and other social networks are key when it comes to fostering an understanding of the advantages universal design and accessible tourism can bring, and helping form a more positive public opinion.

Information provided by television, publishing, and social media will often have a strong influence on how society views persons with disabilities. Unfortunately, in many cases, articles and stories regarding PWDs focus on their disability rather than presenting a positive image of their intellectual and physical abilities. This is another opportunity for education and training—on universal design and the importance of accessible tourism development—to target media professionals, including journalists.

The media can create a new narrative by providing more fact-based and complex material that will help break the unhelpful and often negative stereotypes associated with PWDs.

Stakeholder Mapping

To successfully reach and engage audiences to raise awareness, it is necessary to understand who will benefit from and who has a role in influencing and shaping inclusive environments and accessible tourism.

Stakeholder mapping is a visualization tool that can help

- define stakeholders,
- find new opportunities,
- anticipate challenges and impact,
- plan mitigation strategies,
- define influence and engagement level, and
- plan communication and reporting.[63]

To develop a successful stakeholder mapping, it is important to consider the seven principles of stakeholder management named after Max Clarkson, a dedicated researcher on stakeholder management. It is also important to ensure that the process of stakeholder management is itself accessible and inclusive and supports the involvement and engagement of PWDs.

The seven principles of stakeholder management are:[64]

Principle 1. Acknowledge and actively monitor the concerns of all legitimate stakeholders including persons with disabilities and take their interests appropriately into account in decision-making and operations.

Principle 2. Listen to and openly communicate with stakeholders about their respective concerns and contributions.

Principle 3. Adopt processes and modes of behavior that are sensitive to the concerns and capabilities of each stakeholder.

Principle 4. Recognize the interdependence of efforts and rewards among stakeholders and achieve a fair distribution of the benefits accordingly.

Principle 5. Work cooperatively with public and private entities to reduce negative impacts arising from corporate activities, and where they cannot be avoided, ensure they are appropriately compensated.

---

[63] ADB. 2019. Guidance Note on Stakeholder Communication Strategies for Projects in South Asia. Manila. https://www.adb.org/documents/stakeholder-communication-strategies-projects-guidance-note.

[64] University of Toronto, The Clarkson Center for Business Ethics, Joseph L. Rotman School of Management. 1999. *Principles of Stakeholder Management*. Toronto.

Principle 6. Avoid activities that infringe the rights of stakeholders such as the right to life, property, and clean environment.

Principle 7. Acknowledge potential conflicts and address such conflicts through open and transparent communication and, where necessary, third-party review.

Communication Materials

When preparing communication materials related to disability issues, it will be helpful to ask the following questions:

(i)   What is the purpose of the material?
(ii)   Is the language being used inclusive?
(iii)   Is the material appropriate or showing bias?
(iv)   Has it been considered how the material might affect someone? Is there support available?
(v)   Are any accommodations persons with disabilities might need to participate equally in an activity considered?

When engaging and communicating with PWDs, it is important to be aware of any additional support needs they might have for them to participate equally and fairly. Below are some of the considerations when engaging and communicating with persons with disabilities:

- Ask in advance what additional support needs are required and make suitable arrangements to accommodate individuals in as equal and inclusive way as possible.

- Provide detailed information to all participants in advance to support people in making informed decisions about their own involvement.

- Ensure any venues or places being used are accessible and inclusive (e.g., for events, meetings, and interviews).

- Be able to provide information and materials in alternative formats as required (e.g., large print or in braille).

- Consider the need to provide sign language services or interpretation.

- Consider the need to provide hearing induction loops.

- Ensure any printed or visual content is accessible and inclusive and has subtitles or captions to support people with a hearing impairment.

- Ensure presentations use simple language, are clear and easy to understand, and that presenters speak clearly at an appropriate pace.

- Ensure the presenter or speaker is clearly visible with good lighting to support people who lip read.

- If someone with a speech impairment is misunderstood, ask them to repeat themselves. Do not attempt to guess what they have said or pretend you understand.

3 UNIVERSAL DESIGN STANDARDS

Georgia's Ministry of Economy and Sustainable Development led the development of a National Accessibility Standards to support the country in delivering on the UN's Convention on the Rights of Persons with Disabilities (CRPD).[65] ADB is supporting this process as a development partner. The National Accessibility Standard will act as a tool to enable planners, architects, and designers to create inclusive urban developments and cities. This chapter is considered a precursor to the National Accessibility Standards by providing examples of some of the key areas and issues to be covered.

The universal design standards presented in this chapter intend to support the creation of inclusive outcomes. The historical center of Mtskheta City and the Georgian Parliament Building (as seen in the images below) are good examples of an inclusive infrastructure.

The integration of a shallow gradient provides equal access for people unable to use the steps, including wheelchair users.

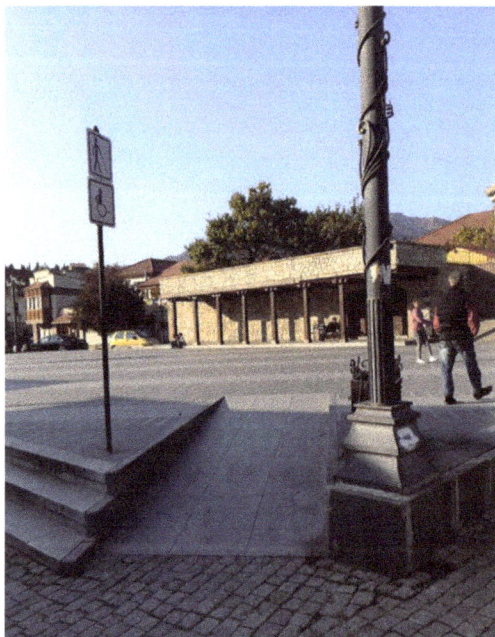

Historical center of city of Mtskheta. The historical center of city of Mtskheta features accessibility ramps (photo by PARSA).

65   Government of Georgia. 2020. Resolution 732 on Technical Regulation: National Accessibility Standards. Tbilisi.

The gradient is very shallow, allowing independent use by most manual wheelchair users and it is directly adjacent to the steps, offering choice and eliminating the need for unnecessary separation between users.

The integration of a lower reception desk with an overhang, supports wheelchair users and people of short stature. It can assist both visitors and staff.

This provides an inclusive experience, often at the point of entry, and thus presents a very good impression for all visitors as they arrive.

Georgian Parliament Building, Tbilisi. Low reception desks inside the Georgian Parliament Building in Tbilisi (photo by Nino Zedginidze / UNDP, The Parliament of Georgia).

Chapter 11 of Resolution No. 41, Technical Regulation of Building Safety Rules requires planning and construction of a building in Georgia to comply with Resolution No. 732 Technical Regulation on National Accessibility Standards. These follow universal design standards. All dimensions are provided in millimeters (mm).

Outdoor Environment

Accessible Routes

Accessible routes are one of the important components of ensuring accessibility in towns and cities.

- The minimum clear width for a wheelchair user and a pedestrian to pass or walk beside each other is 1,800 mm. The minimum clear width for a wheelchair user alone must be 1,200 mm (Figure 15).

- For two wheelchair users to pass, the minimum clear width must be 2,400 mm (Figure 16).
- The accessible route must be level, with no steps and free of obstacles (e.g., protruding, standing, or overhanging objects).
- The surface must be firm and slip-resistant, with no cracks or gaps more than 5 mm wide.

Figure 15: Minimum Clear Width for a Wheelchair User and a Pedestrian to Pass
(millimeters)

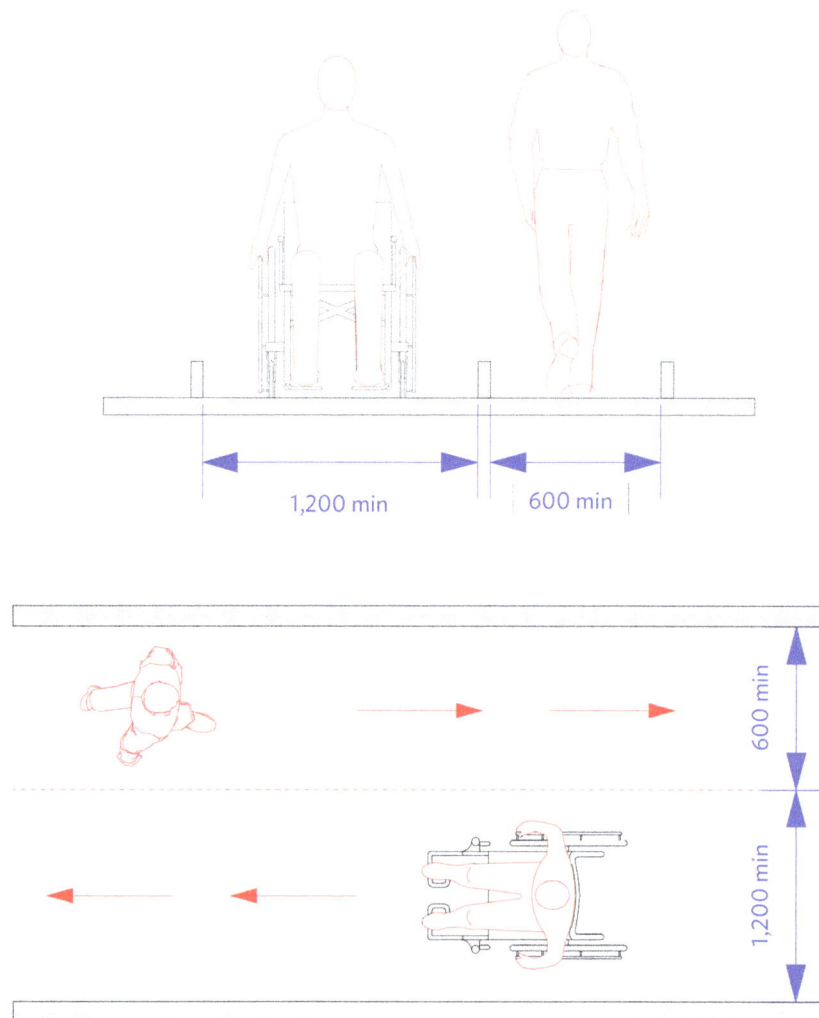

1,200 min   600 min

600 min

1,200 min

min = minimum.
Source: Government of Georgia. 2020. Resolution 732 on Technical Regulation: National Accessibility Standards. Tbilisi.

Figure 16: Minimum Clear Width for Two Wheelchair Users to Pass
(millimeters)

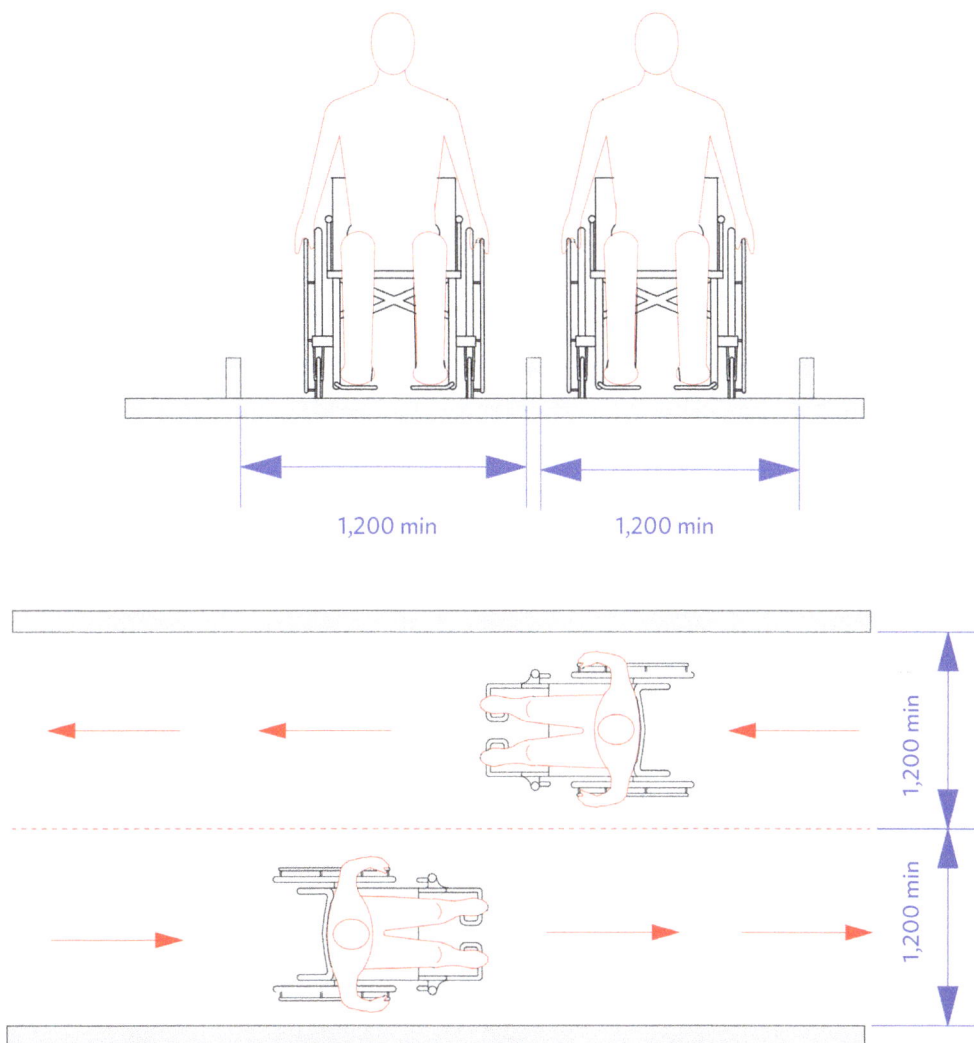

1,200 min   1,200 min

1,200 min

1,200 min

min = minimum.
Source: Government of Georgia. 2020. Resolution 732 on Technical Regulation: National Accessibility Standards. Tbilisi.

Pedestrian Crossings (Crosswalks)

Pedestrian crossings or crosswalks must be clearly identifiable for all users, including people with a visual impairment.

Crosswalks should be marked with contrasting stripes and have a detectable warning surface on the pavement or sidewalk.

Where the crossing meets the pavement, both sides of the roadway should have curb ramps that are accessible for wheelchair users and other mobility device users.

Crossings and curb ramps must be free of obstacles. The curb ramps must also have a detectable warning surface that contrasts tonally with the surrounding pavement surface (e.g., light-on-dark or dark-on-light) and be easily detectable.

Where a controlled pedestrian crossing is provided, traffic light systems should provide audio signals informing pedestrians when it is safe to cross the street.

Curb Ramps

Sidewalk curb ramps are short ramps that cut through a curb or lead up to it. They are an important component of accessible streets, especially for wheelchair users or other mobility device users. They also support people with children in prams and buggies and support people with trolley suitcases, such as tourists.

For the safety of blind people and people with a visual impairment, a detectable warning surface must be provided where the curb ramp meets the roadway. The minimum requirements are as follows:

- The minimum clear width must be 1,200 mm (excluding flared sides and blended transitions).
- Cross-slopes and blended transitions must have a maximum gradient of 1:48.
- Handrails are not required.

Curb ramps and flared sides must be located on traffic lines, access aisles, and parking places. At marked crossings, curb ramps must be contained within the crosswalk, excluding side flares.

Perpendicular curb ramps—top landings. To ensure the connection of an accessible route to the ramp entry point, a landing must be provided at the top of the curb ramp. To ensure a smooth transition between the pavement and the roadway, the curb ramp should be perpendicular to the run of the curb of the pavement (Figure 17). The minimum requirements are as follows:

- The top landing must be a minimum of 1,200 mm x 1,200 mm.
- The cross slope of the landing must be a maximum of 1:48.
- The gradient of the running slope must be a maximum of 1:12.
- Flared sides (intended to prevent tripping hazards) should not exceed 1:10.

Figure 17: Perpendicular Curb Ramp Design
(millimeters)

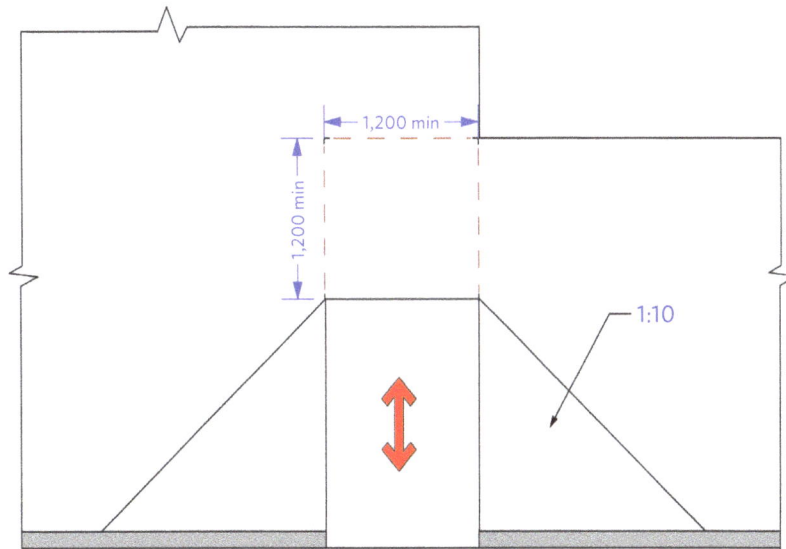

min = minimum.
Source: Government of Georgia. 2020. Resolution 732 on Technical Regulation: National Accessibility Standards. Tbilisi.

Parallel curb ramps. The minimum requirements for parallel curb ramps are as follows:

- For curb ramps parallel to the curb of the pavement, landings a minimum of 1,200 mm x 1,200 mm must be provided at the bottom of the curb ramps (Figure 18).
- The cross slope of the landing must not exceed 1:48.
- The running slope must be a maximum of 1:12.

Figure 18: Parallel Curb Ramp Design
(millimeters)

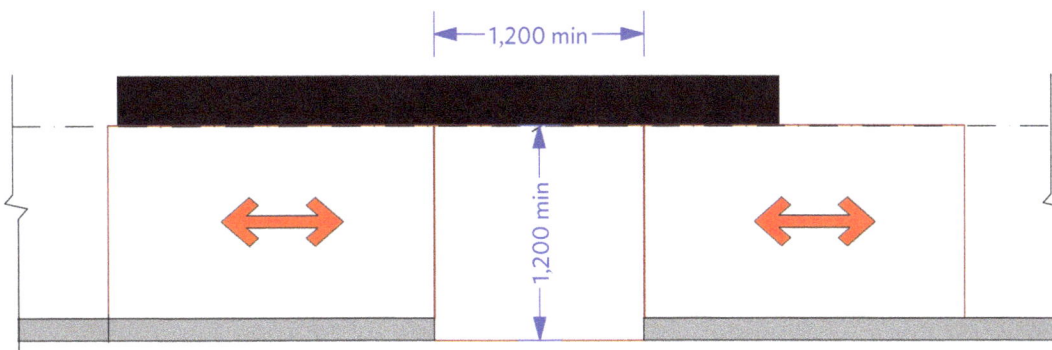

min = minimum.
Source: Government of Georgia. 2020. Resolution 732 on Technical Regulation: National Accessibility Standards. Tbilisi.

Blended transitions. The minimum requirement for blended transitions is a maximum running slope of 1:20 (Figure 19).

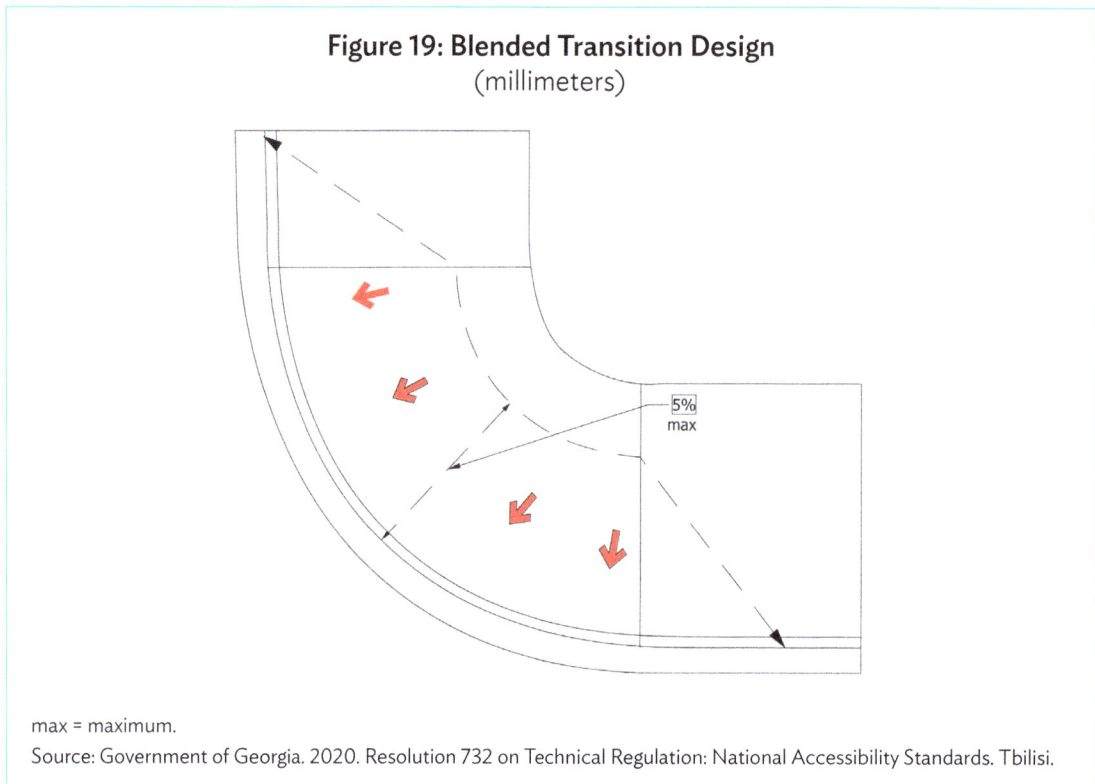

Figure 19: Blended Transition Design
(millimeters)

max = maximum.
Source: Government of Georgia. 2020. Resolution 732 on Technical Regulation: National Accessibility Standards. Tbilisi.

Case Study: Curb Ramps and Detectable Warning Surfaces

Curb ramps are required where level road crossings are not provided. They provide a level route across the road, providing level access to or from the pavement at controlled and uncontrolled crossing points. They are accompanied by a detectable warning surface in the form of blister tactile paving which must have a strong visual contrast with the surrounding ground surface.

Photos by Iain McKinnon.

Detectable Warning Surfaces

Detectable warning surfaces must be provided at curb ramps at crosswalks. They take the form of paving with truncated domes in a color that contrasts with the surrounding pavement surface (e.g., light-on-dark or dark-on-light that is easy to detect). The minimum size requirements for truncated domes are as follows (Figure 20):

- A base diameter of 23 mm minimum and 36 mm maximum.
- A top diameter of 50% minimum and 65% maximum of the base diameter.
- A height of 5.0 mm.

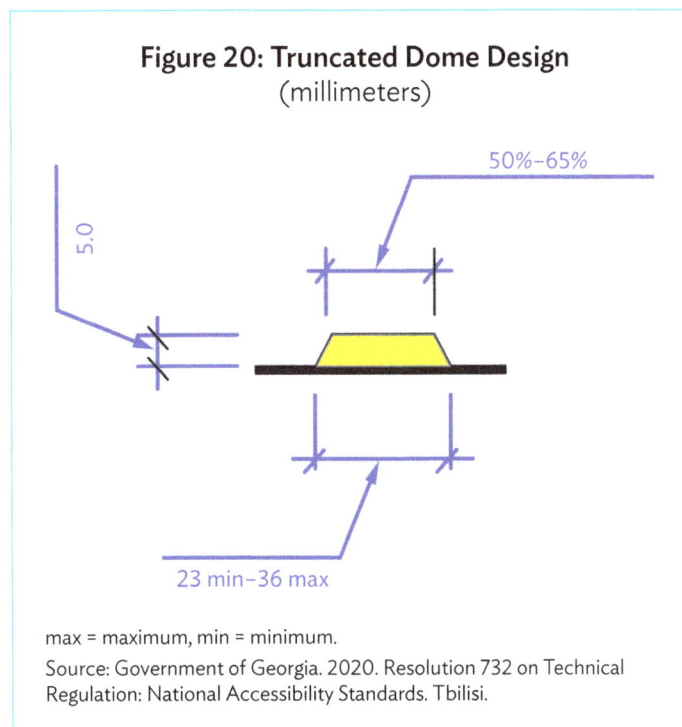

Figure 20: Truncated Dome Design
(millimeters)

50%–65%

5.0

23 min–36 max

max = maximum, min = minimum.
Source: Government of Georgia. 2020. Resolution 732 on Technical Regulation: National Accessibility Standards. Tbilisi.

The spacing of truncated domes is as follows (Figure 21):

- A center-to-center spacing of a minimum of 40 mm and a maximum of 60 mm.
- A base-to-base spacing of a minimum of 16.5 mm (measured between the adjacent domes on the grid).
- Alignment is required to be in a square grid pattern.

Detectable warning surfaces must have a minimum width of 600 mm in the direction of pedestrian travel. At curb ramps and blended transitions, they should extend the full width of the curb ramp run, excluding any flared sides. At boarding platforms for buses and rail vehicles, they should extend the full length of the public use areas of the platform.

Figure 21: Spacing of Truncated Domes
(millimeters)

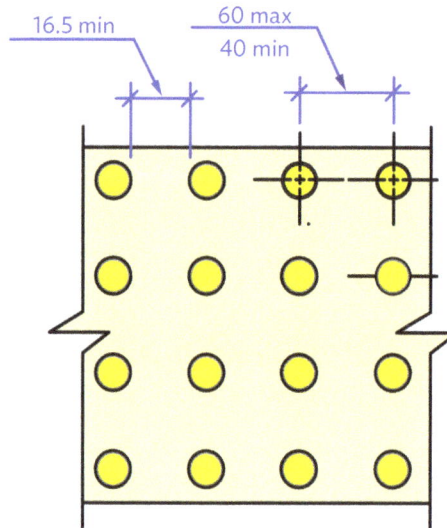

max = maximum, min = minimum.
Source: Government of Georgia. 2020. Resolution 732 on Technical Regulation: National Accessibility Standards. Tbilisi.

Perpendicular curb ramps. At perpendicular curb ramps, detectable warning surfaces must be placed at the bottom of the ramp at the back of the curb. The depth of the warning surface must be a minimum of 600 mm in the direction of pedestrian travel, and the width must be equal to the full width of the curb ramp run, excluding any flared sides (Figure 22).

Figure 22: Detectable Warning Surfaces on Perpendicular Curb Ramps
(millimeters)

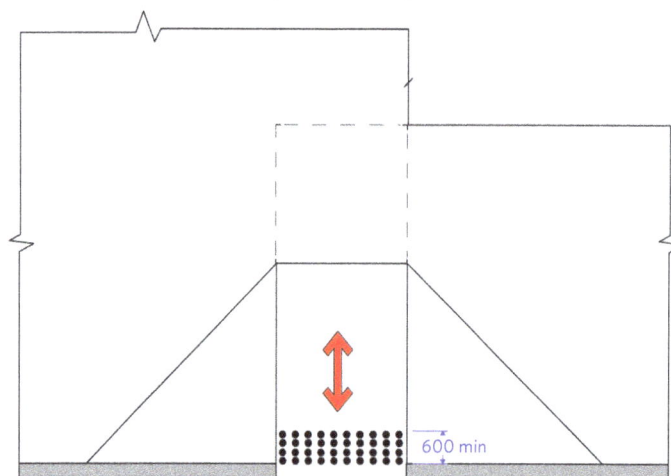

min = minimum.
Source: Government of Georgia. 2020. Resolution 732 on Technical Regulation: National Accessibility Standards. Tbilisi.

Parallel curb ramps. On parallel curb ramps, detectable warning surfaces must be placed on the landing and turning space at the flush transition between the street and sidewalk. The depth of the warning surface must be a minimum of 600 mm. The width must be the full width of the landing and turning space (Figure 23).

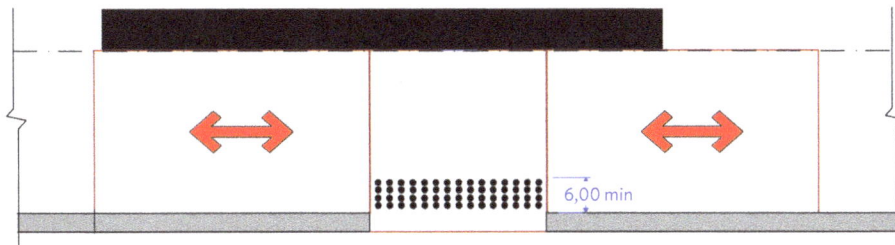

Figure 23: Detectable Warning Surfaces on Parallel Curb Ramps
(millimeters)

6,00 min

min = minimum.
Source: Government of Georgia. 2020. Resolution 732 on Technical Regulation: National Accessibility Standards. Tbilisi.

Blended transitions. Detectable warning surfaces on blended transitions must be placed at the back of curb and must be located along the entire transition (Figure 24).

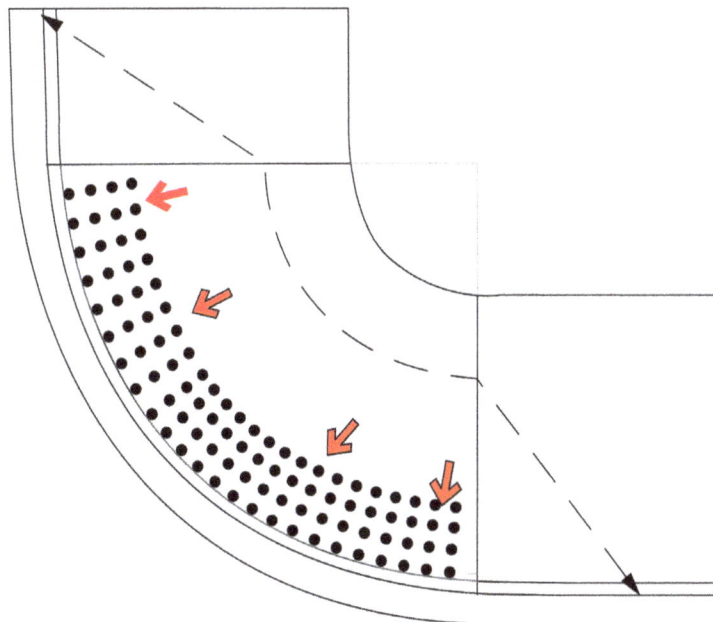

Figure 24: Detectable Warning Surfaces on Blended Transitions
(millimeters)

Source: Government of Georgia. 2020. Resolution 732 on Technical Regulation: National Accessibility Standards. Tbilisi.

Parking Spaces

The provision of parking spaces for persons with disabilities should comply with the requirements in Table 1.

Table 1: Accessible Parking Space Provision

Total Number of Parking Spaces	Required Number of Accessible Parking Spaces
1–25	1
26–50	2
51–75	3
76–100	4
101–150	5
151–200	6
201–300	7
301–400	8
401–500	9
501–1,000	2% of total spaces
1,001 and more	20 spaces are added per 100 spaces

Source: Government of Georgia. 2020. Resolution No. 41 on Approving Technical Regulations for the Safety Rules for Buildings.

The technical specifications for the size of accessible parking spaces are as follows (Figure 25):

- Car parking spaces must have a minimum width of 2,500 mm.
- Van parking spaces must have a minimum width of 3,500 mm.

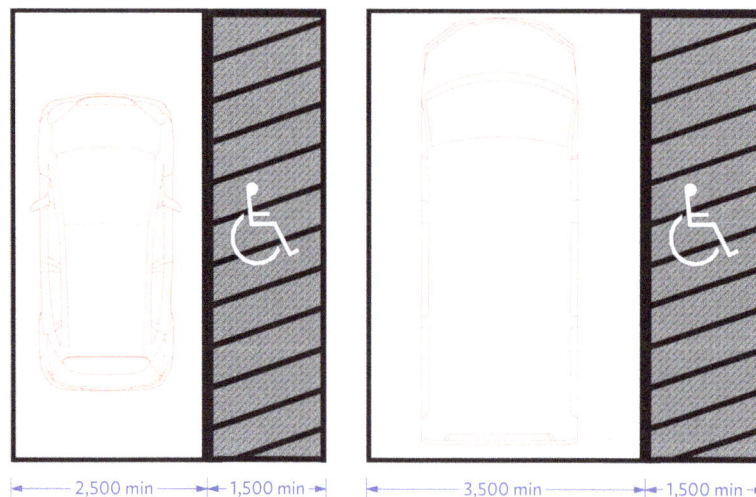

Figure 25: Accessible Parking Space Specifications
(millimeters)

min = minimum.
Source: Government of Georgia. 2020. Resolution 732 on Technical Regulation: National Accessibility Standards. Tbilisi.

Access aisles to parking spaces are required to connect an accessible route. Two parking spaces can share a common access aisle. Parking spaces are permitted to have access aisles placed on either side of the car or van parking space and should not overlap with the vehicle space. Where van parking spaces are angled, there must be access aisles on the passenger side of the parking space.

- Access aisles for car and van parking spaces must have a minimum width of 1,500 mm.
- Access aisles must extend the full length of the parking spaces.

Parallel parking spaces. Where the width of the adjacent sidewalk is more than 4,300 mm, an access aisle must be a minimum of 1,500 mm wide, and the length must be the full length of the parking space. An access aisle is required to connect to a pedestrian access route (Figure 26).

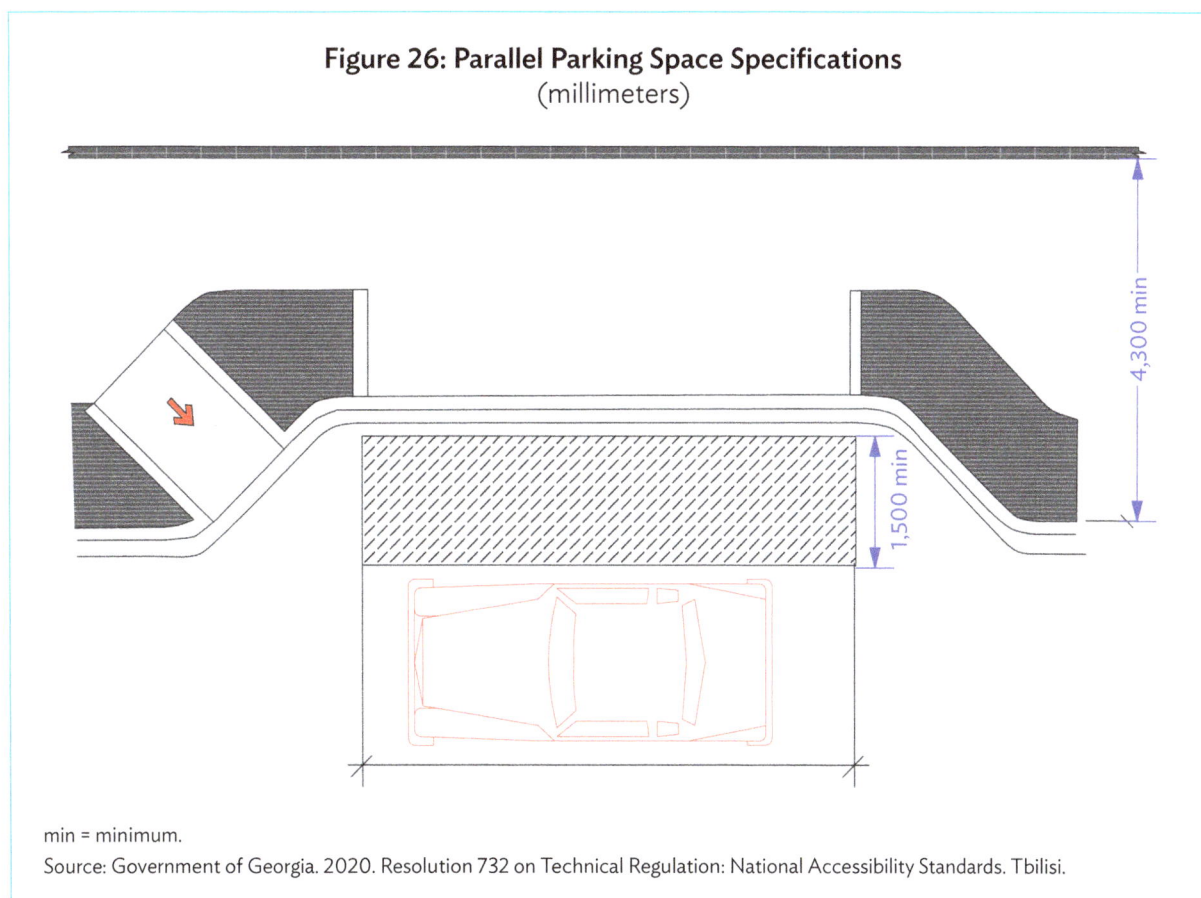

Figure 26: Parallel Parking Space Specifications
(millimeters)

min = minimum.
Source: Government of Georgia. 2020. Resolution 732 on Technical Regulation: National Accessibility Standards. Tbilisi.

Perpendicular or angled parking spaces. Access aisle on perpendicular or angled parking must be a minimum of 2,500 mm wide and the length must be the full length of the parking space. An access aisle is required to connect to a pedestrian access route. Two parking spaces can share a common access aisle (Figure 27).

Figure 27: Angled Parking Space Specifications
(millimeters)

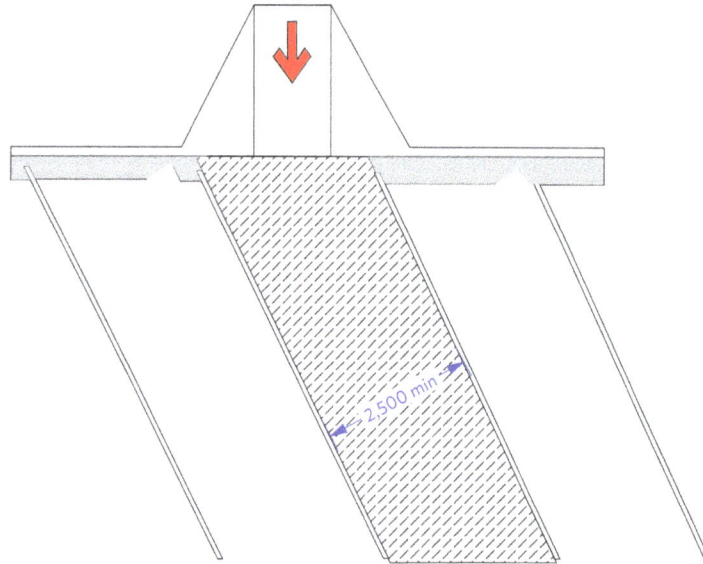

min = minimum.
Source: Government of Georgia. 2020. Resolution 732 on Technical Regulation: National Accessibility Standards. Tbilisi.

Case Study: Parking Spaces

Accessible parking spaces are essential as many disabled people will rely on the car to get around. They should always be located as close as possible to the main entrance of the building. Access aisles should be provided between accessible parking spaces. It is also good practice to provide clear space to the rear of the parking space to give a dedicated and protected space to retrieve items from the rear of the car.

Photos by Iain McKinnon.

Public Transport

Public transport hubs, stops, and station locations should be spread across the city to be equally accessible to the inhabitants of its different districts.

Stops. Important arrangements to be made at the stops are as follows:

- No steps should be needed to get to the stops.
- If needed, elevators or ramps should be arranged to allow people to reach their destination, but riders should not be required to seek alternate paths from other patrons just to find an accessible route.
- There should not be any barriers at the main route.
- If terminals require people to travel long distances, moving walkways and rest areas are important to help decrease fatigue while getting to destinations within the station.

Payment and gates. Specifications for payment machines and gates are as follows:

- Payment machines must be arranged to make them easy to reach and use for people in both a seated and standing position.
- Gates must include an accessible option that is wide enough to accommodate wheelchair users.
- Payment machines and gates should be located on the primary pathway used to reach a destination.
- Contrasting markings and simple, clear instructions should be provided to make payment machines and gates easier to see, use, and understand.
- For more convenience, staff can be placed in high-traffic areas to assist riders with the process.
- Payment machines should have raised characters and braille.

Shelters and seating. Outdoor shelters are important part of the transport infrastructure, as they not only ensure the safety of those waiting, but also provide protection from the weather (rain, snow, or extreme heat). Specifications are as follows:

- Shelters should include benches or seats to rest and should include floor space for wheelchair users directly adjacent to the bench or seat.
- Benches should provide both back and arm rests to give additional support to people who need it.
- The interior of buses and trains should be designed with wide aisles and extra floor space.

Train or tram platforms. Contrasting colors, tactile changes, and lighting can be used to indicate the platform's edge. There should be a minimal gap between the platform and the vehicle for safety. Floor space inside a vehicle should provide adequate space for mobility equipment users and those with strollers and luggage. To ensure safety while in motion, enough place should be provided for holding on, including low and high options for anyone sitting or standing.

Bus boarding and alighting areas. The minimum requirements are as follows:

- Boarding and alighting areas at bus stops must be a minimum of 2,500 mm clear length, measured perpendicular to the curb or vehicle roadway edge, and a minimum of 1,500 mm clear width measured parallel to the vehicle roadway (Figure 28).
- The slope of the bus stop boarding and alighting area perpendicular to the vehicle roadway must not exceed 1:48.
- Bus stop boarding and alighting areas must be connected to streets, sidewalks, or pedestrian paths by an accessible route.
- Bus shelters must have enough clear floor space for waiting passengers, including wheelchair users.

Information and signage. Information and signage about stations, routes, and destinations must be provided in clearly legible characters. Lists of stations, routes, and destinations served by the station, platforms, or stops must be marked with visual characters. Signage information should also be provided as raised characters and in braille.

Figure 28: Bus Boarding and Alighting Area Specifications
(millimeters)

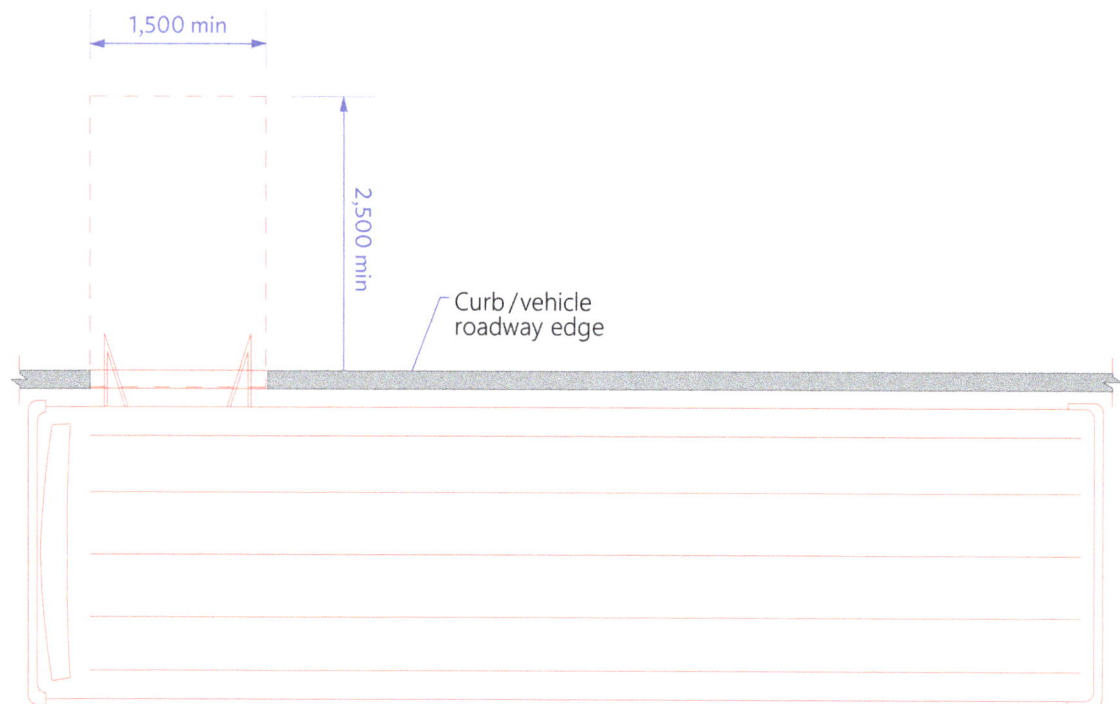

1,500 min

2,500 min

Curb / vehicle roadway edge

min = minimum.
Source: Government of Georgia. 2020. Resolution 732 on Technical Regulation: National Accessibility Standards. Tbilisi.

Case Study: Public Transport

For public transport to be accessible requires both accessible infrastructure (i.e., stops and platforms) and also accessible vehicles (i.e., buses and trains). Both examples below are from London, UK and demonstrate a bus stop and shelter with access to a bus via an automatic ramp and also the Docklands Light Railway (DLR) which provides direct level access between platforms and trains.

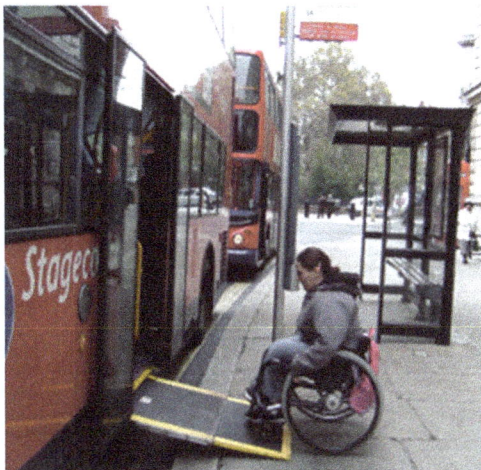

Photo by mobilitysolutions.co.uk.

Photo by intelligenttransport.com.

Ramps

The minimum requirements for ramps are as follows:

- The running slope must not be steeper than 1:12.
- The cross slope must be a maximum of 1:48.
- The clear width must be a minimum of 900 mm. Handrails and handrail fittings provided on the ramp run must not project into the required clear width of the ramp run.
- The rise for any ramp run must be a maximum of 750 mm.
- Ramps must have level landings at the bottom and top of each ramp run with a clear width of at least the width of the widest ramp run leading to the landing.
- The landing clear length must be a minimum of 1,500 mm.
- The landing cross slope must be a maximum of 1:48.
- At change of direction, and between runs, intermediate landings must be provided, with minimum dimensions of 1,500 mm x 1,500 mm (Figure 29).
- Ramp runs with a rise greater than 150 mm should have handrails on both sides.
- Side protection measuring at least 100 mm high is required to keep any mobility device on the ramp. Side protection must prevent the passage of a 100-mm diameter sphere.

Figure 29: Ramp Specifications
(millimeters)

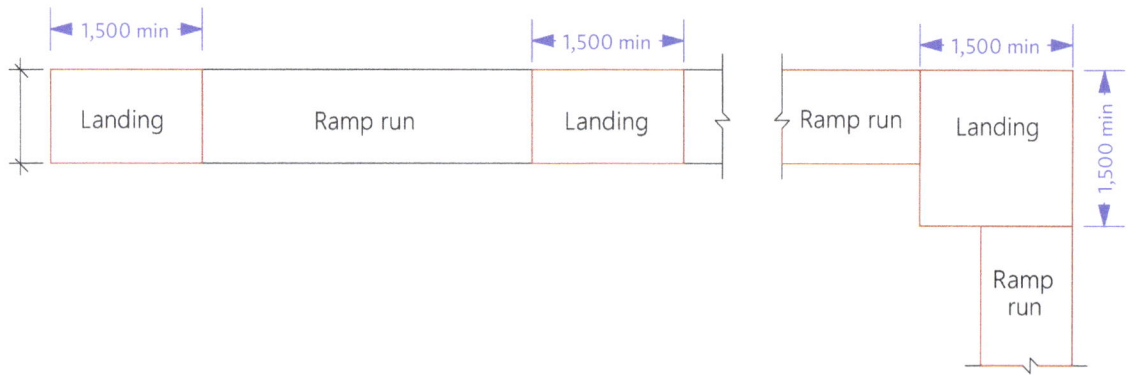

min = minimum.
Source: Government of Georgia. 2020. Resolution 732 on Technical Regulation: National Accessibility Standards. Tbilisi.

Handrails on Ramps and Stairs

The minimum requirements for handrails on ramps and stairs are as follows:

- Handrails must be provided on both sides of stairs and ramps.
- Handrails must be continuous within the full length of each stair flight or ramp run.
- Gripping surfaces must be continuous, not interrupted by other construction elements or obstructions.
- There must be no sharp abrasive elements on handrails and adjacent wall surfaces.
- Handrails must be securely fixed, not rotating within their fittings.
- Ramp handrails must extend horizontally above the landing, a minimum of 300 mm beyond the top and bottom of ramp runs (Figure 30).
- Handrail height must be a minimum of 860 mm and a maximum of 1,000 mm.

Figure 30: Handrail Specifications for Ramps and Stairs
(millimeters)

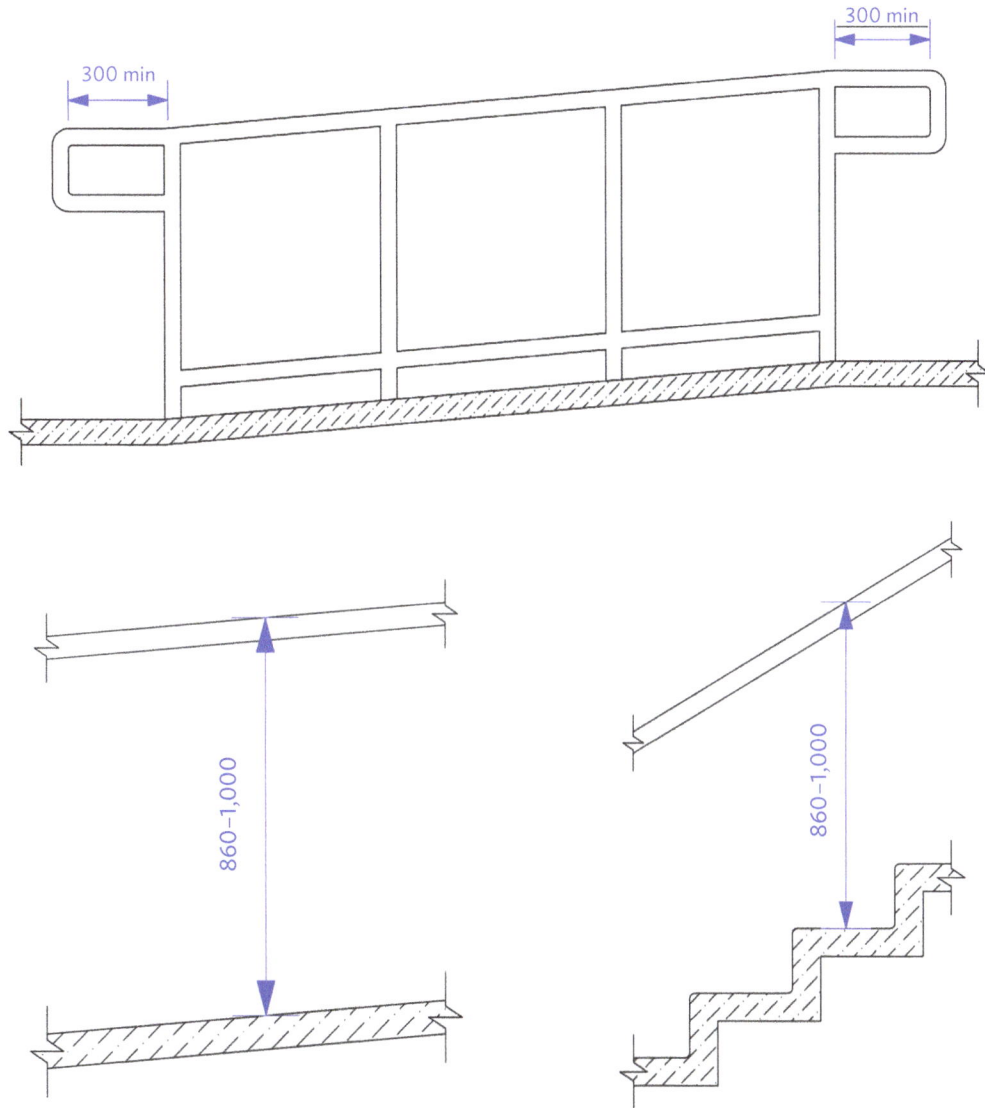

Source: Government of Georgia. 2020. Resolution 732 on Technical Regulation: National Accessibility Standards. Tbilisi.

Case Study: Handrails on Ramps and Stairs

Handrails should be comfortable to grip and be continuous on both stairs and ramps. They should extend horizontally at the head and foot of both stairs and ramps and then also finish in a positive end (i.e., return to ground) as not to trap or snag users' clothing.

Photos by Iain McKinnon.

Indoor Environment

Floor Surfaces

The minimum requirements for floor surfaces are as follows:

- Floor surfaces must be stable, firm, and slip-resistant.
- Openings in floor surfaces (i.e., for drainage) must not permit the passage of a 13-mm diameter sphere.
- Changes in level must not be permitted within the turning space.
- The turning space must be circular with a minimum diameter of 1,700 mm.

Protruding Objects

When planning and designing ramp runs and landings (Figures 29 and 30), indoor and outdoor, consideration must be given to ensure they do not present any hazard to people with a visual impairment. For example, care should be taken to prevent the projection of objects, such as handrails, into circulation paths including interior and exterior walkways, paths, hallways, and courtyards.

Protruding objects between a height range of 680 mm and 2,050 mm above the floor may only protrude horizontally a maximum of 100 mm into a circulation path (Figure 31).

Figure 31: Protruding Object Specifications
(millimeters)

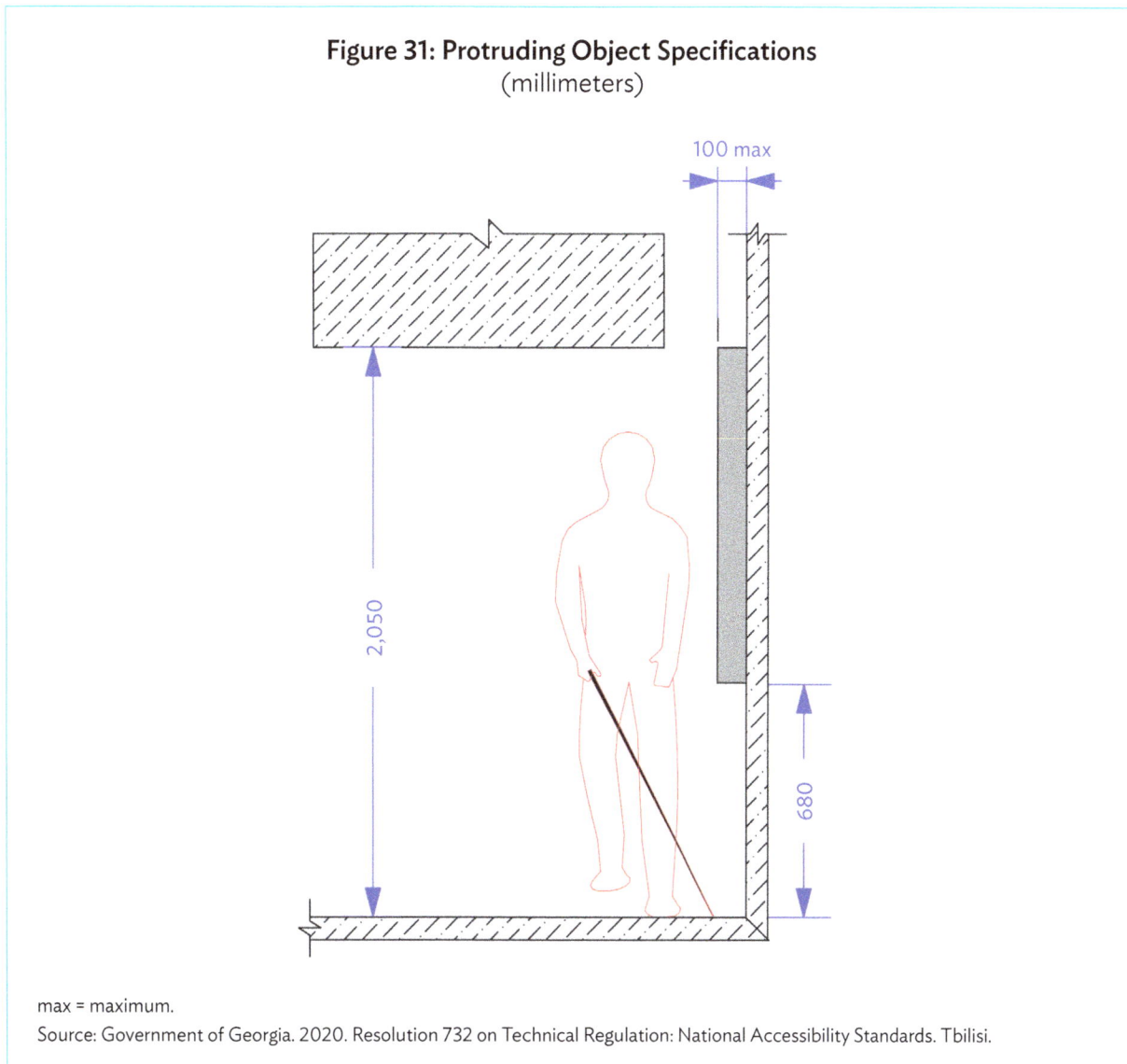

max = maximum.
Source: Government of Georgia. 2020. Resolution 732 on Technical Regulation: National Accessibility Standards. Tbilisi.

Reach Ranges

Minimum requirements for reach ranges are as follows:

- For unobstructed reach, the high forward reach must be a maximum of 1,200 mm above the floor and the low forward reach must be a minimum of 380 mm above the floor (Figure 32).

Figure 32: Specifications for Unobstructed Reach
(millimeters)

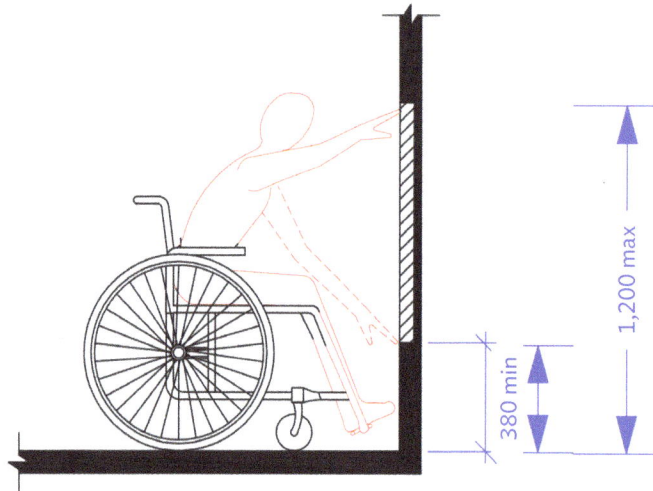

max = maximum, min = minimum.
Source: Government of Georgia. 2020. Resolution 732 on Technical Regulation: National Accessibility Standards. Tbilisi.

When a high forward reach is over an obstruction. Where the reach depth over the obstruction is a maximum of 500 mm, the high forward reach must be a maximum of 1,200 mm above the floor (Figure 33).

Figure 33: Specifications for High Forward Reach over an Obstruction
(millimeters)

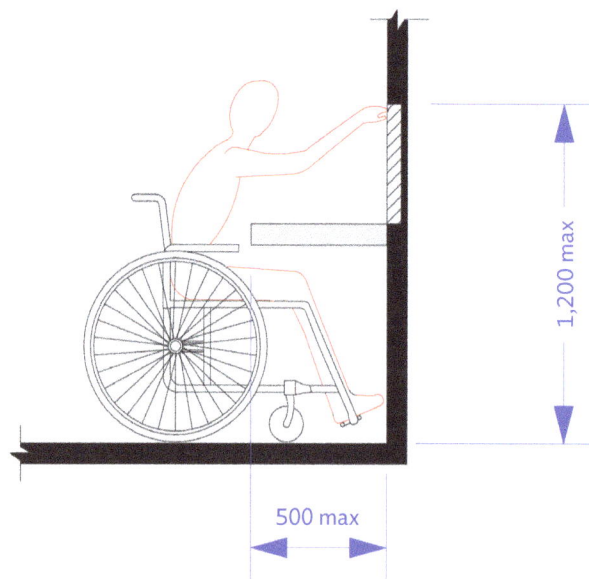

max = maximum.
Source: Government of Georgia. 2020. Resolution 732 on Technical Regulation: National Accessibility Standards. Tbilisi.

Where the reach depth over the obstruction is greater than 500 mm and not more than 630 mm, the high forward reach must be a maximum of 1,100 mm above the floor (Figure 34).

Figure 34: Specifications for High Forward Reach over a Larger Obstruction
(millimeters)

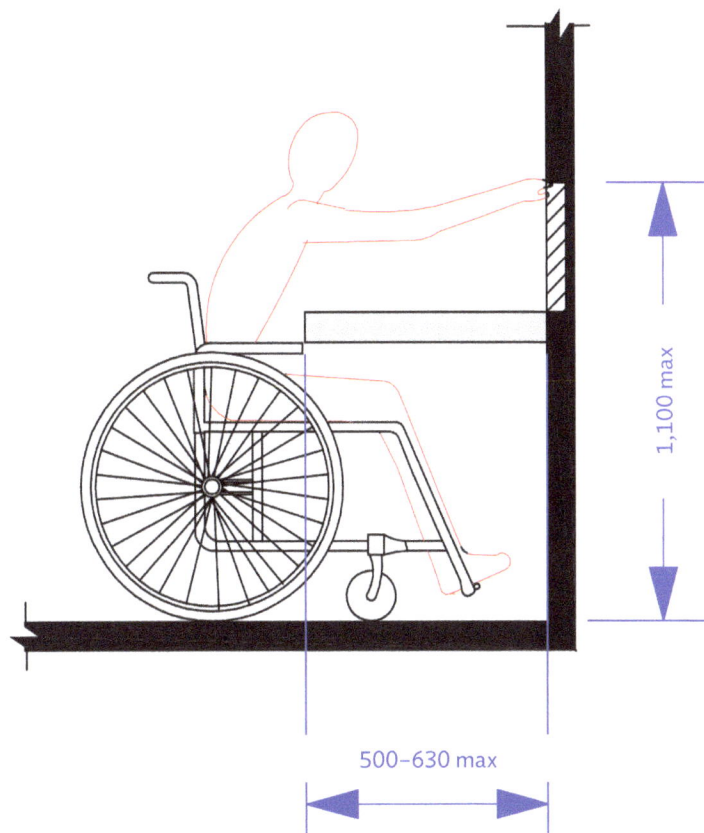

1,100 max

500–630 max

max = maximum.
Source: Government of Georgia. 2020. Resolution 732 on Technical Regulation: National Accessibility Standards. Tbilisi.

Side Reach

The minimum requirements for side reach are as follows:

- For unobstructed reach, when a clear floor space permits parallel approach to an element and the edge of the clear floor space is a maximum of 250 mm from the element, the high side reach must be a maximum of 1,200 mm above the floor and the low side reach must be a minimum of 380 mm above the floor (Figure 35).

Figure 35: Unobstructed Side Reach Specifications
(millimeters)

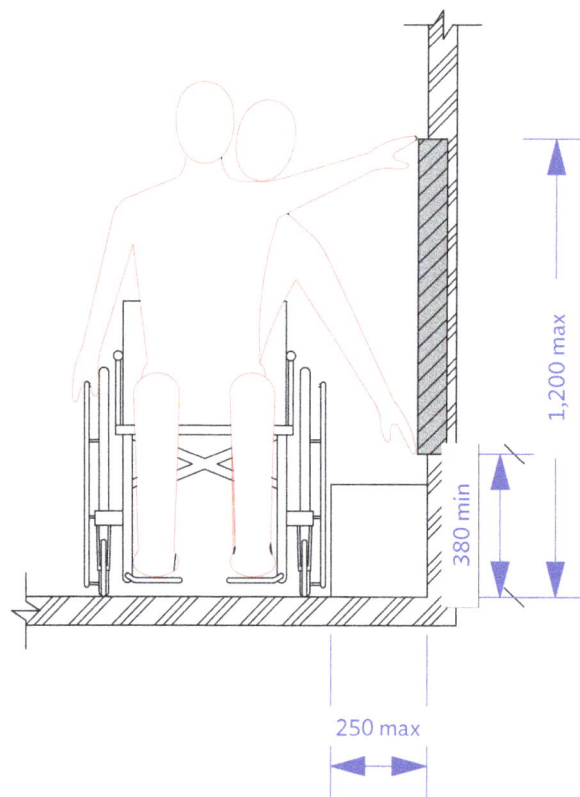

max = maximum, min = minimum.
Source: Government of Georgia. 2020. Resolution 732 on Technical Regulation: National Accessibility Standards. Tbilisi.

For obstructed high side reach, the following specifications apply:

- The high side reach must be a maximum of 1,170 mm from the floor, considering an obstruction 860 mm above the floor at a depth of between 250 mm and a maximum of 600 mm from the wall (Figure 36a).

Figure 36a: Obstructed High Side Reach Specifications
(millimeters)

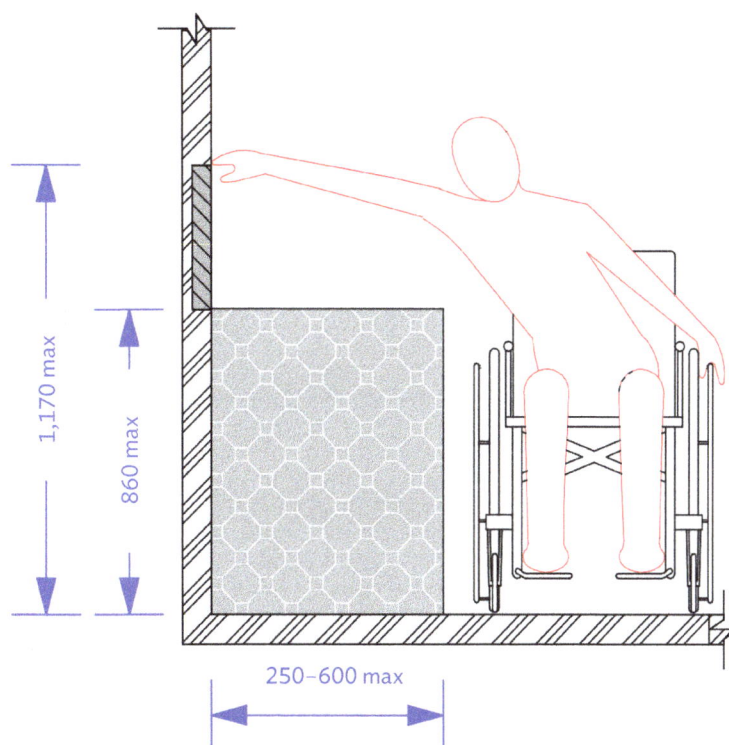

1,170 max

860 max

250–600 max

max = maximum.
Source: Government of Georgia. 2020. Resolution 732 on Technical Regulation: National Accessibility Standards. Tbilisi.

For a maximum reach depth of 250 mm, the high side reach must be a maximum of 1,200 mm above the floor (Figure 36b).

Figure 36b: Obstructed High Side Reach Specifications
(millimeters)

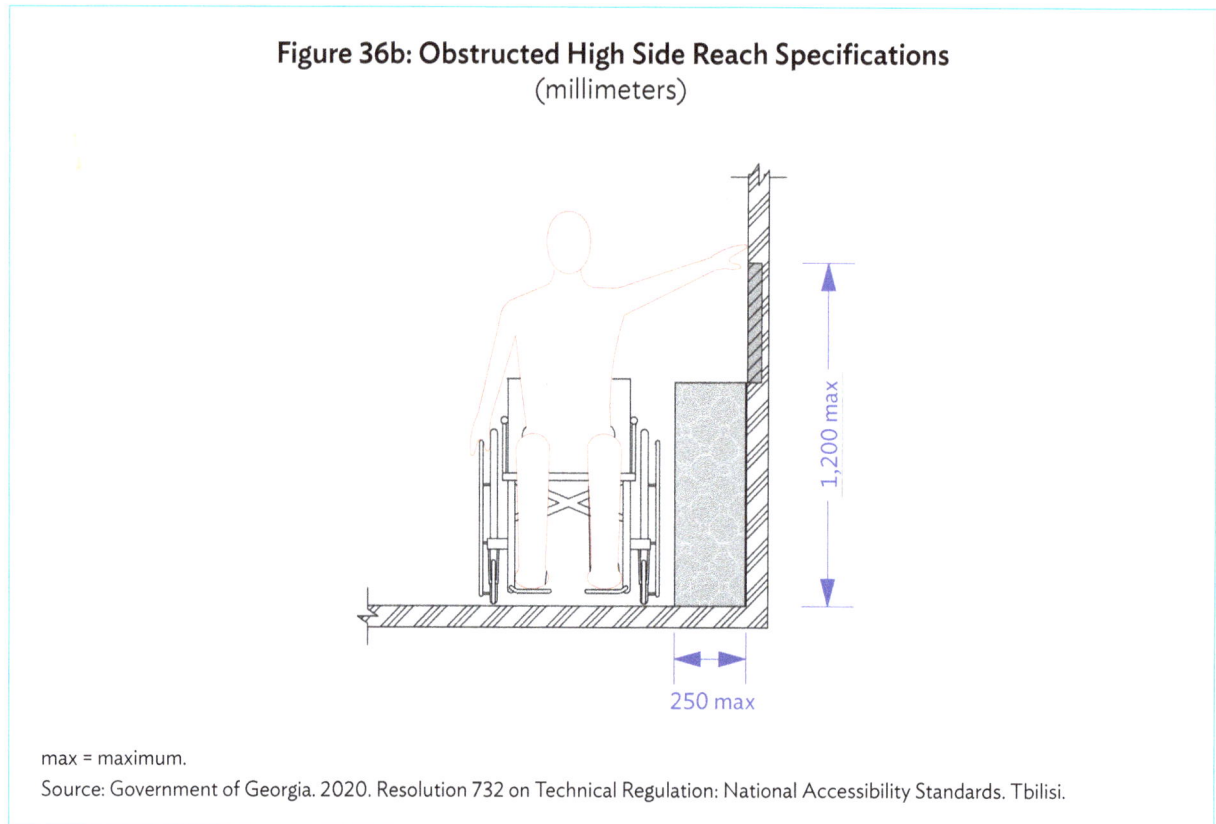

1,200 max

250 max

max = maximum.
Source: Government of Georgia. 2020. Resolution 732 on Technical Regulation: National Accessibility Standards. Tbilisi.

Interior Accessible Routes

Interior accessible routes include corridors, doors and gates across corridors, ramps, and access to lifts. The minimum interior accessible route requirements are as follows:

- Interior accessible routes to accommodate one wheelchair user must be a minimum of 900 mm wide (Figure 37).
- Interior accessible routes to allow a wheelchair user to comfortably pass a pedestrian should be a minimum of 1,500 mm wide (Figure 37).
- Interior accessible routes to allow two wheelchair users to pass each other should be a minimum of 1,800 mm wide (Figure 38).
- Accessible routes must be free of obstructions, steps, and protruding objects.
- Surfaces must be stable, firm, and slip-resistant.

Figure 37: Interior Accessible Route Specifications
(millimeters)

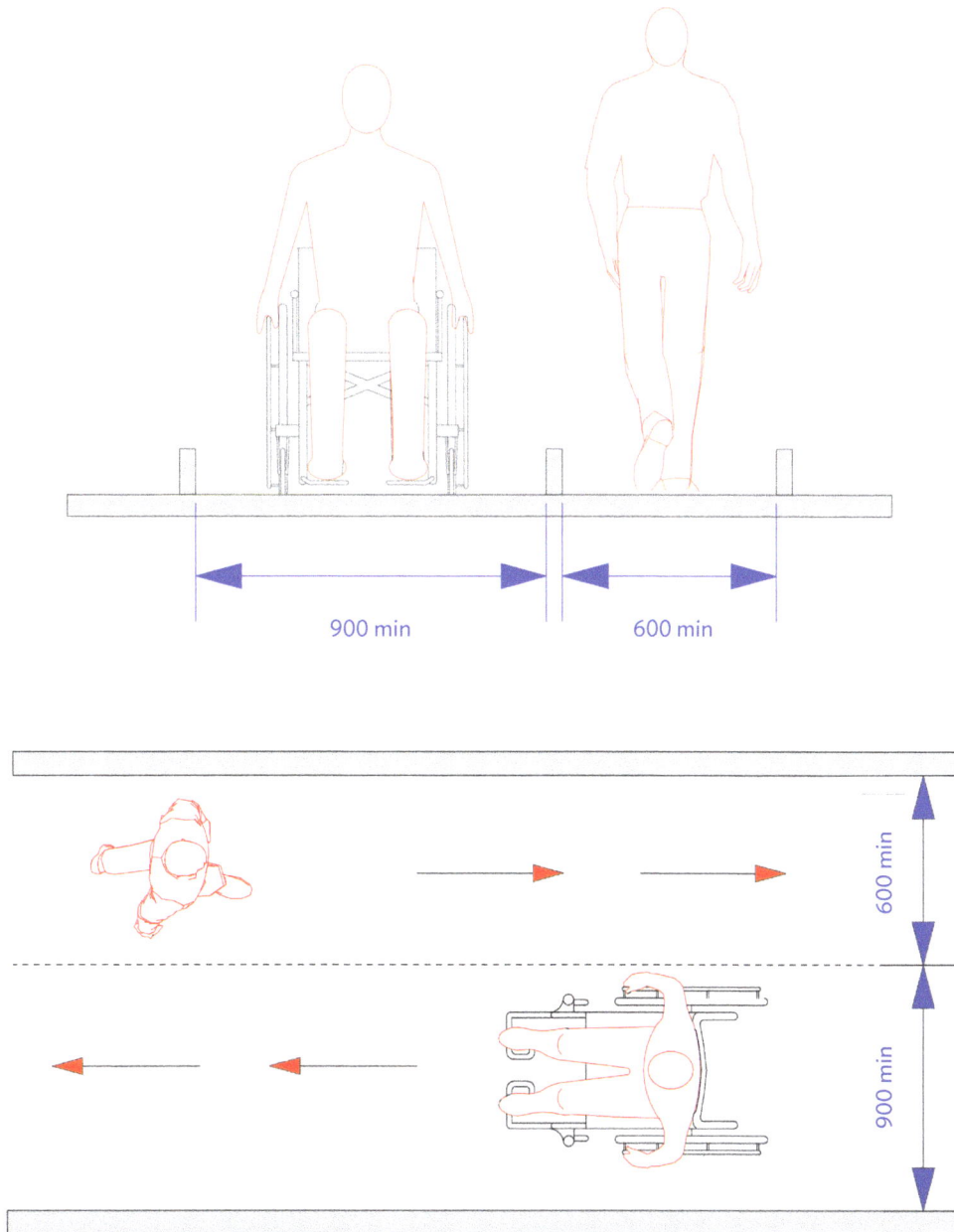

900 min

600 min

600 min

900 min

min = minimum.

Source: Government of Georgia. 2020. Resolution 732 on Technical Regulation: National Accessibility Standards. Tbilisi.

Figure 38: Interior Accessible Route Specifications for Two Wheelchair Users to Pass
(millimeters)

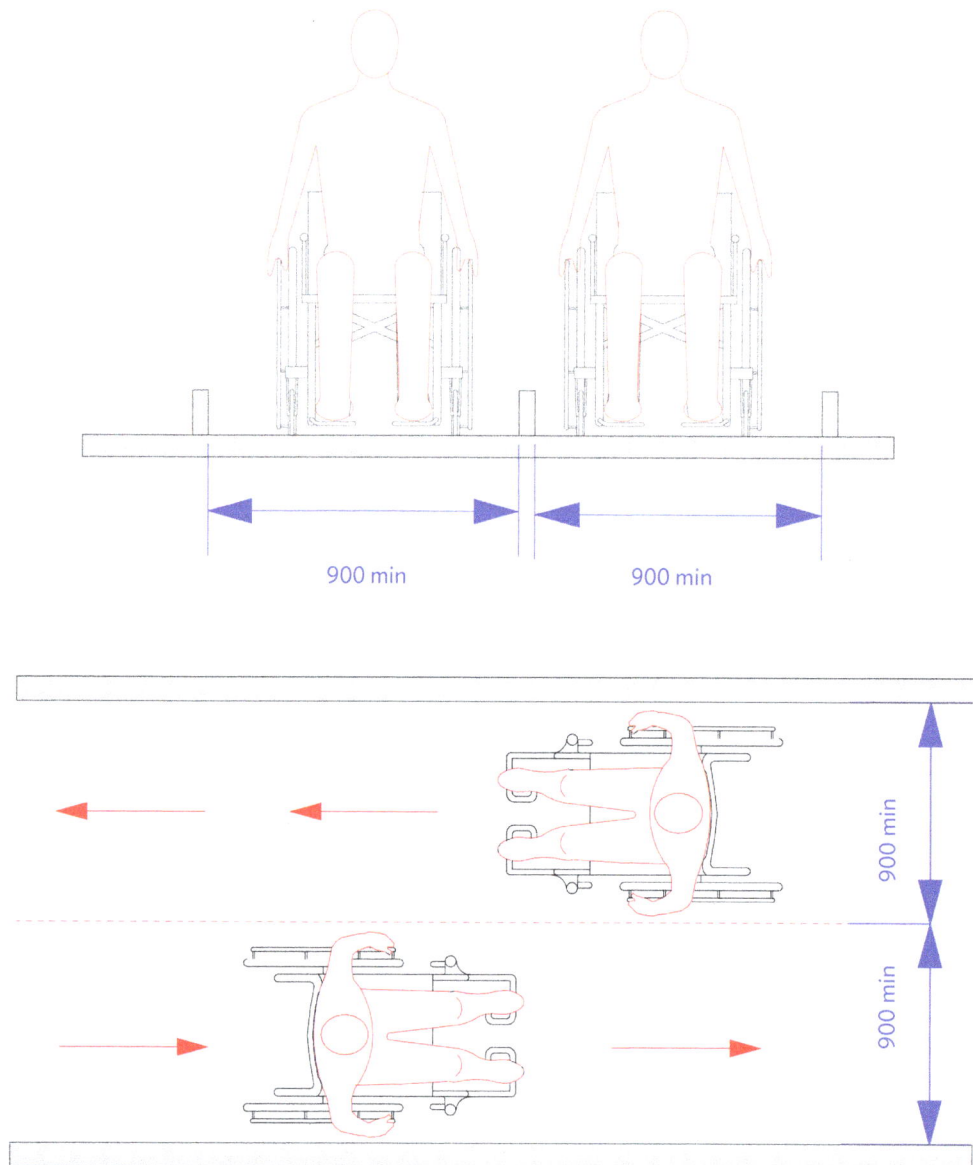

900 min   900 min

900 min

900 min

min = minimum.
Source: Government of Georgia. 2020. Resolution 732 on Technical Regulation: National Accessibility Standards. Tbilisi.

Entrances and Doors

The minimum requirements for entrances and doors are as follows:

- The clear width of the interior door must be a minimum of 820 mm.
- Doors must be easy to open and close, and must not require tight grasping, pinching, or twisting of the wrist to operate.
- The operable parts of hardware must be a minimum of 860 mm and a maximum of 1,200 mm above the floor.
- Glass doors must have safety markings to make them noticeable.

Case Study: Entrances and Doors

Main entrances must be clearly obvious on the approach. Ideally, entrance doors will be automatically power operated, sliding double door sets. Where doors are glazed, they should have manifestations (safety markings) to support people with a visual impairment.

Photos by noviniti.co.uk.

Wayfinding and Signage

Good, clear signage is often an important part of creating an accessible environment. The minimum requirements for signs are as follows:

Visual characters

- Sentence case characters should be used as most people recognize a word by its shape when written in a sentence case (i.e., capital first letter with the rest of the word in lower case).
- Fonts used should be clearly legible and sans serif (i.e., Arial).
- Text should not be in italics, oblique, highly decorative, or in other unusual formats.
- Characters and their background should not have glare finish.
- Characters must contrast with the background with either light characters on a dark background, or dark characters on a light background.

Raised characters

Where signage is in positions where people with a visual impairment are likely to touch read (i.e., office doors), providing raised signage (embossed) text can be helpful for many people.

- Raised characters must be a minimum of 0.8 mm above their background.
- They must also comply with the visual characters recommended above.

Braille

Where signage is in positions where people with a visual impairment are likely to touch read (i.e., office doors, on equipment), providing braille can be helpful for many people. The minimum requirements for braille are as follows (Figure 39):

- Braille should correspond to the text. If the text is multiline, the braille must be placed directly below the text it corresponds to.
- For wall mounted signs, for braille to be used effectively, it should be located between 1,200 mm and 1,500 mm above the floor, measured to the baseline of the braille cells.

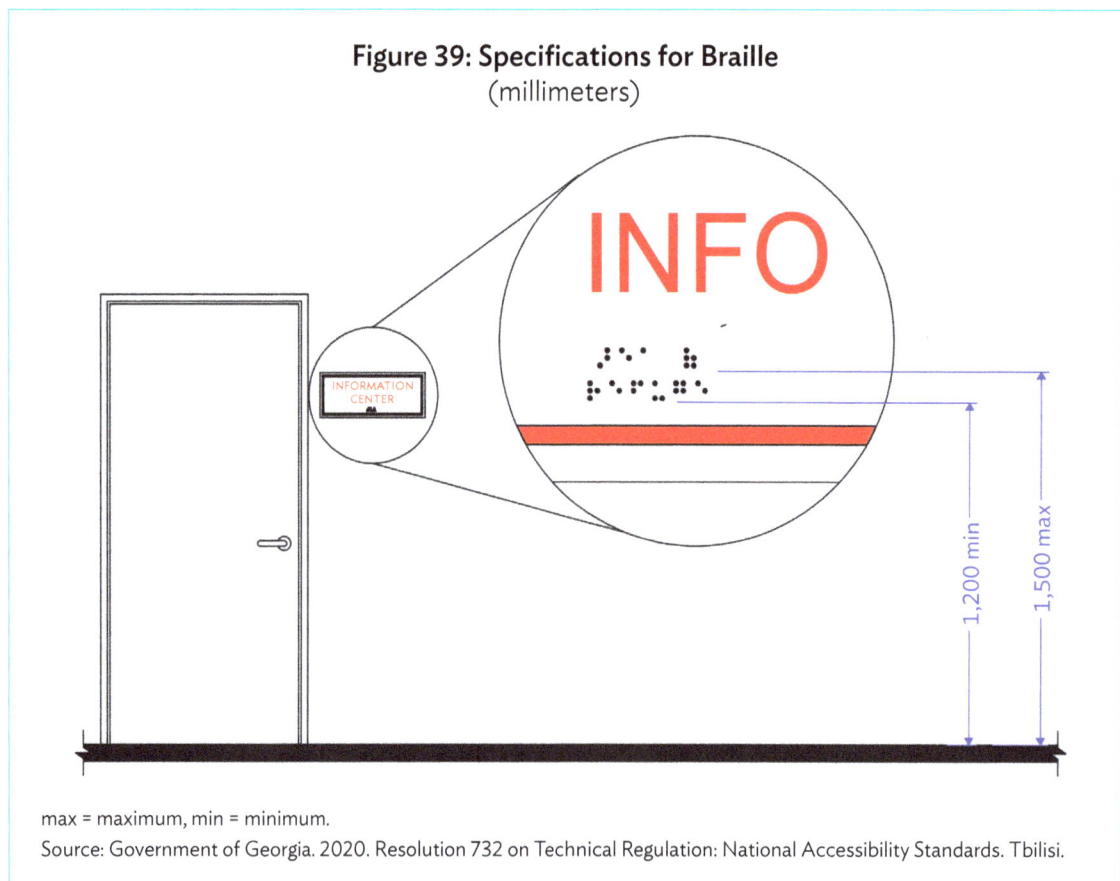

Figure 39: Specifications for Braille
(millimeters)

max = maximum, min = minimum.
Source: Government of Georgia. 2020. Resolution 732 on Technical Regulation: National Accessibility Standards. Tbilisi.

Signage location

- Any sign containing raised characters and braille at a door must be beside the latch side of the door and not on the door itself.

- Any sign containing raised characters and braille at double doors with one active leaf must be located on the inactive leaf.

- If there is a sign containing raised characters and braille at double doors with two active leaves, the sign should be to the right of the right-hand door.

- If there is no wall space on the latch side of a single door or to the right side of double doors, signs must be on the nearest adjacent wall.

- Characters and their background should not have glare finish. Characters must contrast with the background with either light characters on a dark background, or dark characters on a light background.

- Raised characters must be a minimum of 1,200 mm above the floor, measured to the base of the lowest raised character, and a maximum of 1,500 mm above the floor, measured to the base of the highest raised character (Figure 40).

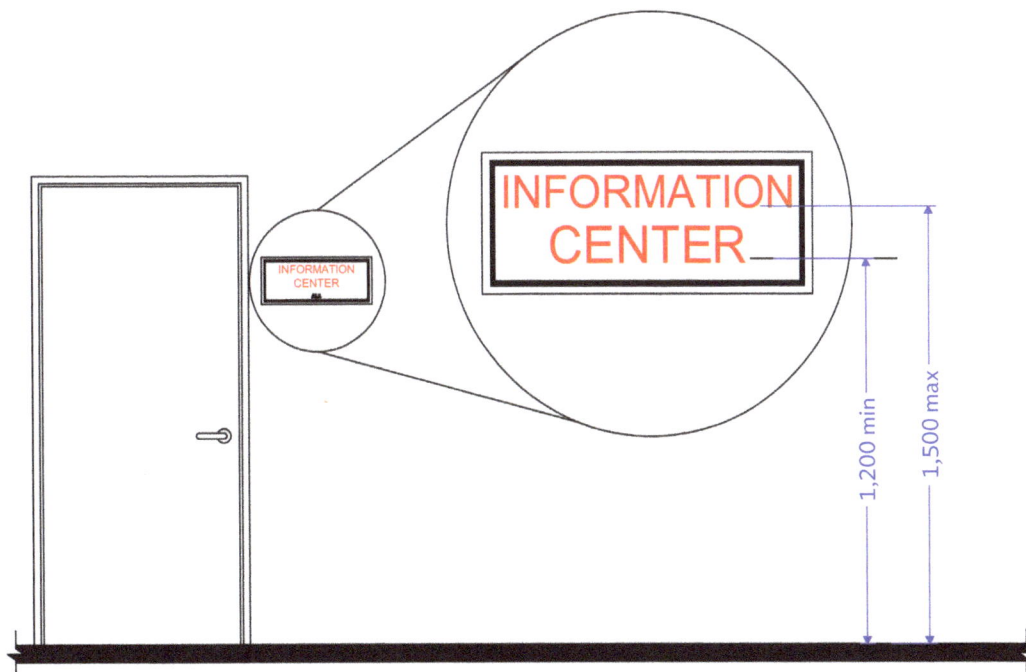

Figure 40: Location Specification for Signs
(millimeters)

max = maximum, min = minimum.
Source: Government of Georgia. 2020. Resolution 732 on Technical Regulation: National Accessibility Standards. Tbilisi.

Pictograms

The use of pictograms and symbols is encouraged as they are often more recognizable and they support people who speak different languages. Therefore, this is helpful when considering tourist attractions where there are likely to be many different language speakers. The minimum requirements for pictograms are as follows:

- **Height.** Large signage pictograms should be at least 150 mm tall. Characters or braille must not be in the pictogram field.
- **Finish and contrast.** Pictograms must not have a glare finish and must contrast visually with their backgrounds, with either a light pictogram on a dark background or a dark pictogram on a light background.

Case Study: Wayfinding and Signage

Signage can be used to support wayfinding. It is important that wayfinding is intuitive and does not solely rely on signage. Symbols and pictograms should accompany text. This supports many neurodiverse people and also people who speak a different language (i.e., international visitors). Signage should be simple and consistent to give people confidence that they are going the right way.

Photos by Iain McKinnon.

Elevators

Elevators are often the easiest way for individuals—in particular, for people with a mobility impairment—to move between floors in multilevel buildings and are, therefore, the preferred means of providing step-free access.

- Elevators must be located on accessible routes.
- Elevators for public use must be large enough to accommodate the intended number of users, including wheelchair users, people with young children in prams and buggies, and people carrying luggage.
- Directional signs to locate elevators must be easy-to-read and displayed throughout all routes inside a facility.
- Both audio and visual signal of the elevator's direction of movement and announcement of stops must be provided.

Elevator controls

The minimum requirements for elevator control buttons are as follows:

- The size of call buttons must be a minimum of 20 mm diameter.
- A clear floor space must be provided at call controls.
- The call button designating the up direction must be located above the one designating the down direction.
- Call buttons must have visible and audible signals to indicate when each call is registered and when each call is answered.
- Call buttons and keypads must be placed between a range of 380 mm and a maximum of 1,200 mm above the floor (Figure 41).
- All control buttons must have raised characters and braille.

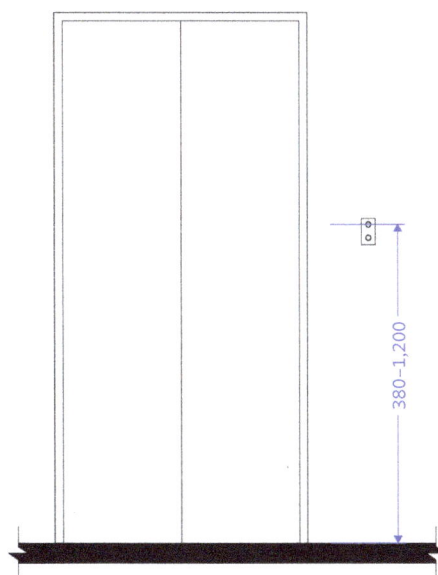

Figure 41: Height of Elevator Call Buttons
(millimeters)

380–1,200

Source: Government of Georgia. 2020. Resolution 732 on Technical Regulation: National Accessibility Standards. Tbilisi.

Elevator Doors

The minimum requirements for elevator doors are as follows:

- Elevator doors must be automatic sliding doors.
- The dimensions of the clear, level maneuvering space in front of an elevator door must be a minimum of 1,500 mm x 1,500 mm.
- To ensure safe maneuvering, the distance between the elevator entrance and the stairs located on the opposite side must be a minimum of 2,000 mm.

The minimum dimensions of elevator cars must comply with the dimensions given in Table 2.

Table 2: Minimum Dimension of Elevator Cars

Door Location	Door Clear Opening Width (in mm)	Inside Car, Back Wall to Inside Face (in mm)	Inside Car, Side to Side (in mm)	Inside Car, Back Wall to Front Return (in mm)
Centered	1,000	1,370	2,000	1,290
Side (off-center)	900	1,370	1,700	1,290
Other	900	2,000	1,370	2,000
Other	900	1,500	1,500	1,500

mm = millimeter.
Source: Government of Georgia. 2020. Resolution 732 on Technical Regulation: National Accessibility Standards. Tbilisi.

Case Study: Elevators

Elevators (or passenger lifts) are the preferred way to change levels for people unable to use stairs and are a better solution than platform lifts. Elevators should be obvious on the approach and be sized to accommodate anticipated crowd flow. Consideration should be given to fire-rated elevators that can be used in an emergency evacuation as part of the fire escape strategy.

Photos by Iain McKinnon.

Platform Lifts

Platform lifts can be used in situations where an elevator is not possible, for example, in some historic buildings with building constraints.[66] However, it should be noted that platform lifts are often less reliable and can be challenging to use for many persons with disabilities. The minimum requirements for platform lifts are as follows:

- Doors must remain open for a minimum of 20 seconds.
- On lifts with one door on a narrow end and one door on a long side, the end door clear opening width must be a minimum of 820 mm. The side door clear opening width must be 1,000 mm.
- Ramp widths must not be less than the platform opening they serve.
- Platform lifts with a single door or doors on opposite ends shall provide a minimum clear floor width of 900 mm and a minimum clear floor depth of 1,300 mm.
- Platform lifts with doors on adjacent sides must provide a minimum clear floor width of 1,100 mm and a minimum clear floor depth of 1,500 mm.
- Control buttons must have raised characters and braille.

Accessible Toilets

Accessible toilets must be designed for independent use, meeting the requirements of persons with disabilities. Many other users can benefit from the provision of accessible toilets, such as those with short-term impairments during recovery after an illness or medical treatment. The minimum requirements for accessible toilets are as follows:

- The accessible toilet must be easily located within a short walking distance.
- The door to the accessible toilet must be clearly marked with the International Symbol of Accessibility.
- The minimum area of a wheelchair accessible toilet compartment must be 1,500 mm in the width measured perpendicular to the side wall, and a minimum of 1,400 mm in depth for wall hung water closets, and minimum of 1,500 mm in depth for floor mounted water closets perpendicular to the rear wall.
- Where an alternate wheelchair accessible toilet compartment is provided, the minimum area of the compartment must be a minimum of 1,500 mm in width, perpendicular to the side wall, and a minimum of 2,150 mm in depth perpendicular to the rear wall.
- The accessible toilet must be equipped with an alarm system.
- Doors must not swing into the clear floor space.
- If sufficient space is not provided in the accessible toilet, the door must open outwards.

---

[66]   Resolution No. 41 - Technical Regulation on Building Safety Rules, Resolution 732 on Technical Regulation: National Accessibility Standards and ASME A18.1 Safety Standards for Platform Lifts.

Water closet (Toilet)

The minimum requirements for water closets are as follows:

- The toilet must be located with a wall or partition to the rear and to one side.
- The centerline of the toilet must be a minimum of 400 mm and a maximum of 450 mm from the side wall or partition.
- The height of the toilet must be a minimum of 430 mm and a maximum of 480 mm from the floor.

Grab bars

The minimum requirements for grab bars are as follows:

- A horizontal grab bar with a minimum length of 1,070 mm must be located a maximum of 300 mm from the rear wall and extend a minimum of 1,370 mm from it.
- The length of a vertical grab bar must be a minimum of 450 mm.
- The bottom of the vertical grab bar must be located a minimum of 990 mm and a maximum of 1,040 mm above the floor.
- The fixed rear-wall grab bar must have a minimum length of 900 mm, located a maximum of 170 mm from the sidewall and extend a minimum of 1,070 mm from the sidewall (Figure 42).

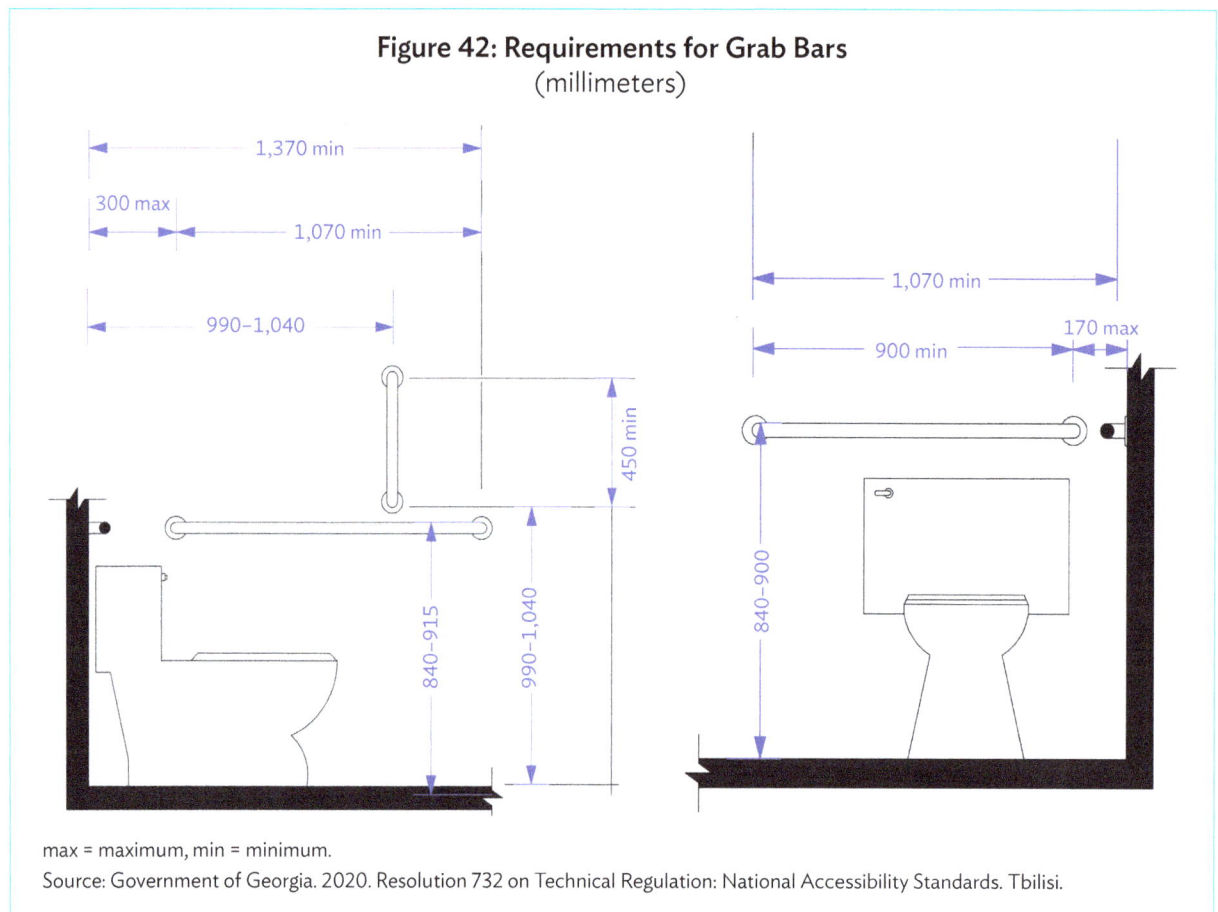

Figure 42: Requirements for Grab Bars
(millimeters)

max = maximum, min = minimum.
Source: Government of Georgia. 2020. Resolution 732 on Technical Regulation: National Accessibility Standards. Tbilisi.

Dispensers

The minimum requirements for dispensers are as follows:

- For dispensers located above the grab bar, the outlet of the dispenser must be located within an area that is a minimum of 600 mm and a maximum of 900 mm from the rear wall (Figure 43).
- For dispensers located below the grab bar, the outlet of the dispenser must be located a minimum of 450 mm and a maximum of 1,200 mm above the floor.

Figure 43: Requirements for Dispensers
(millimeters)

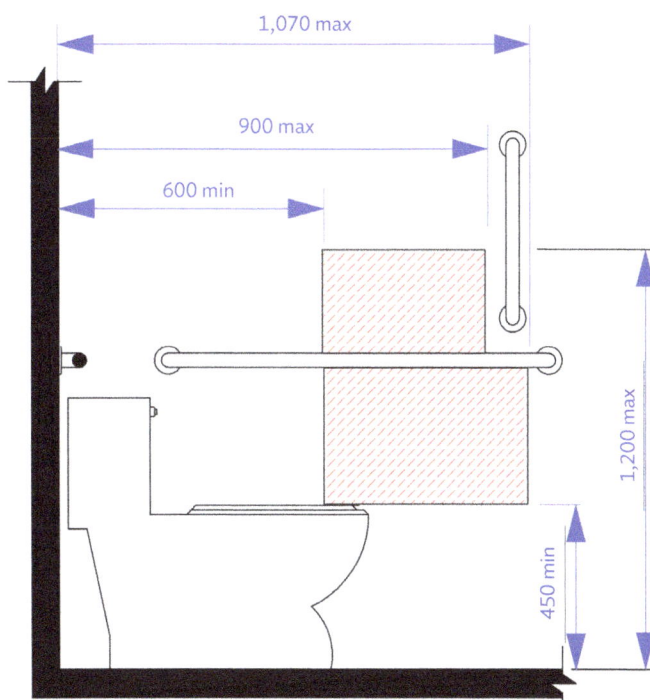

max = maximum, min = minimum.
Source: Government of Georgia. 2020. Resolution 732 on Technical Regulation: National Accessibility Standards. Tbilisi.

Washbasins and sinks

The minimum requirement for washbasins and sinks is as follows:

- The washbasin or sink must be a maximum of 860 mm above the floor (Figure 44).

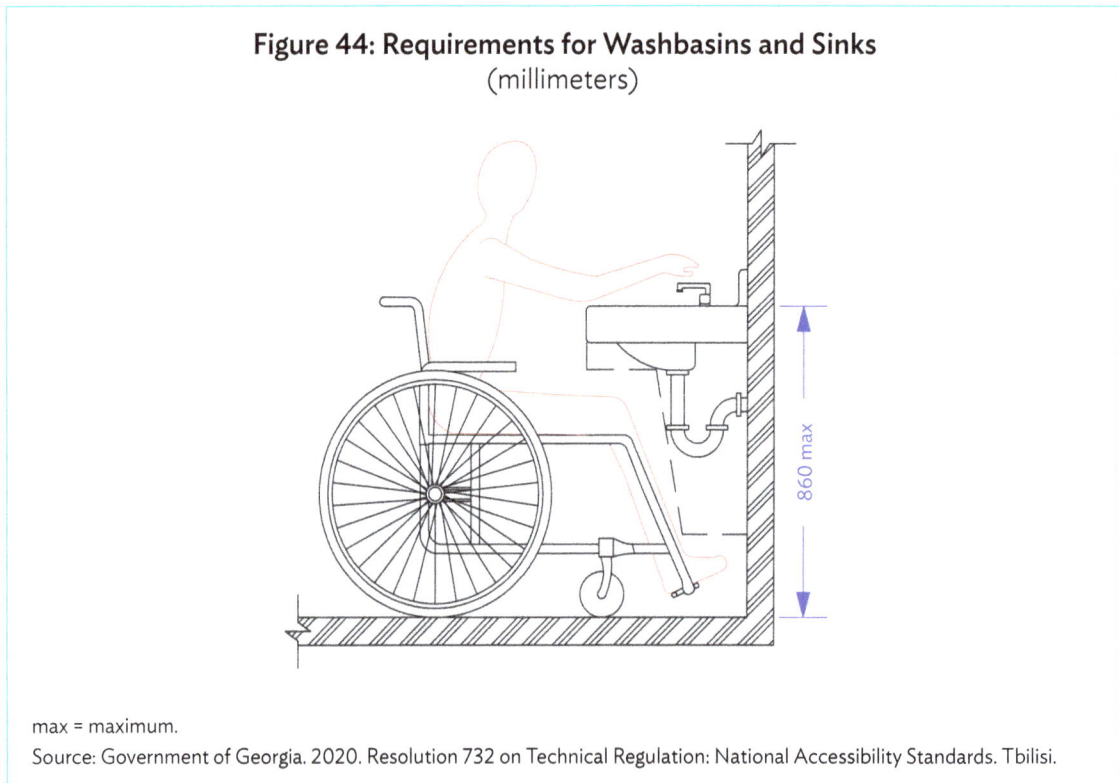

Figure 44: Requirements for Washbasins and Sinks
(millimeters)

860 max

max = maximum.
Source: Government of Georgia. 2020. Resolution 732 on Technical Regulation: National Accessibility Standards. Tbilisi.

Accessories

The minimum requirements for accessories are as follows:

- Soap, towel, and other accessories must be placed within reach range. Water and soap outlets must be provided at a maximum reach depth of 280 mm.
- The bottom edge of the mirror above the lavatory must be located at a maximum of 1,000 mm from the floor.
- Coat hooks provided within toilet compartments must be a maximum of 1,200 mm above the floor.
- Shelves must be a minimum of 1,000 mm and a maximum of 1,200 mm above the floor.

Case Study: Accessible Toilets

Accessible toilets should be provided wherever male and female toilets are provided to be inclusive. Accessible toilets should be decorated to the same standards and aesthetic as male and female toilets and not a lesser standard. In large public buildings where people may spend a long time, consideration should be given to large accessible toilets that support assisted use (called Changing Places toilets in the UK).

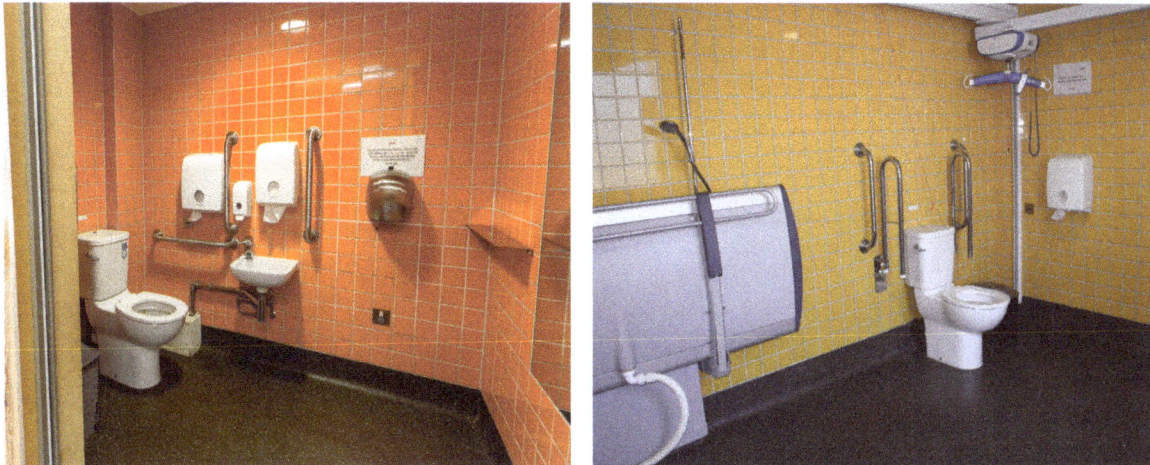

Photos by Iain McKinnon.

Alarms

- An assistance alarm that can be reached from changing or shower seats, from the toilet and by a person lying on the floor, must be made available in all accessible toilets. The alarm must be connected to an emergency help point where a member of staff can provide assistance.

Bathtubs

Clearance

- The clearance in front of a bathtub that extends its length must be 760 mm wide (Figure 45).
- If a permanent seat is placed at the head end of the bathtub, the clearance must extend at least 300 mm beyond the wall at the head end of the bathtub (Figure 46).

Figure 45: Clearance Requirement in Front of Bathtubs
(millimeters)

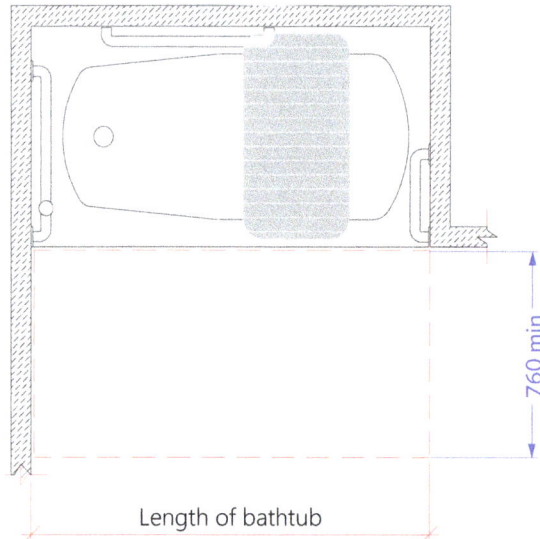

760 min

Length of bathtub

min = minimum.
Source: Government of Georgia. 2020. Resolution 732 on Technical Regulation: National Accessibility Standards. Tbilisi.

Figure 46: Clearance Requirement in Front of Bathtubs with Permanent Seats
(millimeters)

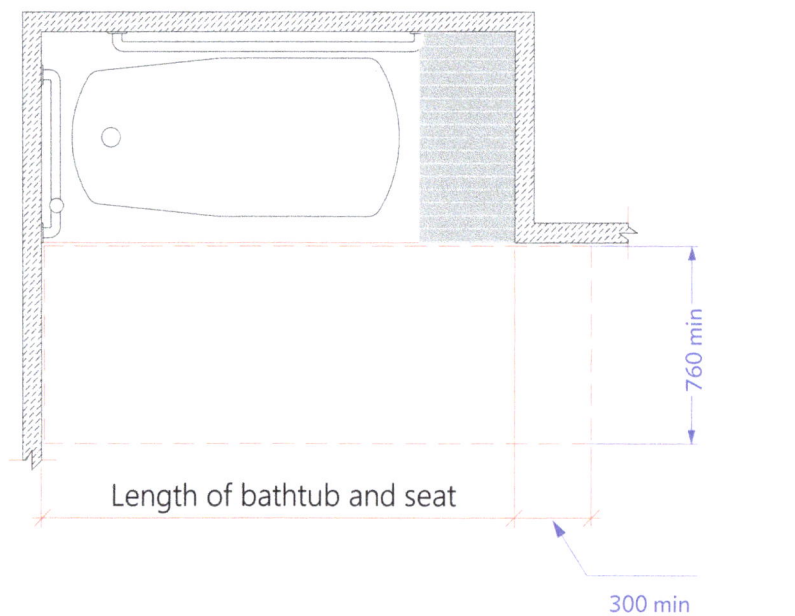

760 min

Length of bathtub and seat

300 min

min = minimum.
Source: Government of Georgia. 2020. Resolution 732 on Technical Regulation: National Accessibility Standards. Tbilisi.

Bathtubs with permanent seats

Back wall

- Two horizontal grab bars must be installed on the back wall above the rim of the bathtub. They must be at least 200 mm and a maximum 250 mm above the rim of the bathtub (Figure 47).
- Each grab bar must be placed a maximum of 380 mm from the head-end wall and extend a maximum of 300 mm from the control-end wall (Figure 49).
- **Horizontal grab bar.** A horizontal grab bar at least 600 mm long must be placed on the control-end wall. The bar must begin near the front edge of the bathtub and extend to the inside corner of the bathtub.
- **Vertical grab bar.** A vertical grab bar that is at least 450 mm long must be installed on the control end wall above the horizontal grab bar, a minimum of 75 mm and a maximum of 150 mm inward from the front edge of the bathtub (Figure 47).

Figure 47: Positioning of Horizontal and Vertical Grab Bars in Bathtubs (Elevation)
(millimeters)

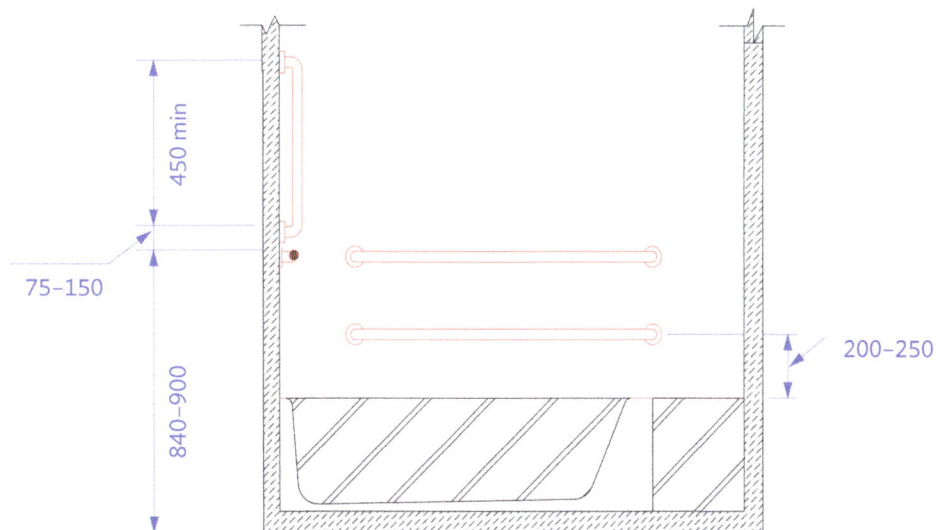

min = minimum.
Source: Government of Georgia. 2020. Resolution 732 on Technical Regulation: National Accessibility Standards. Tbilisi.

Figure 48: Positioning of Horizontal and Vertical Grab Bars in Bathtubs (Plan)
(millimeters)

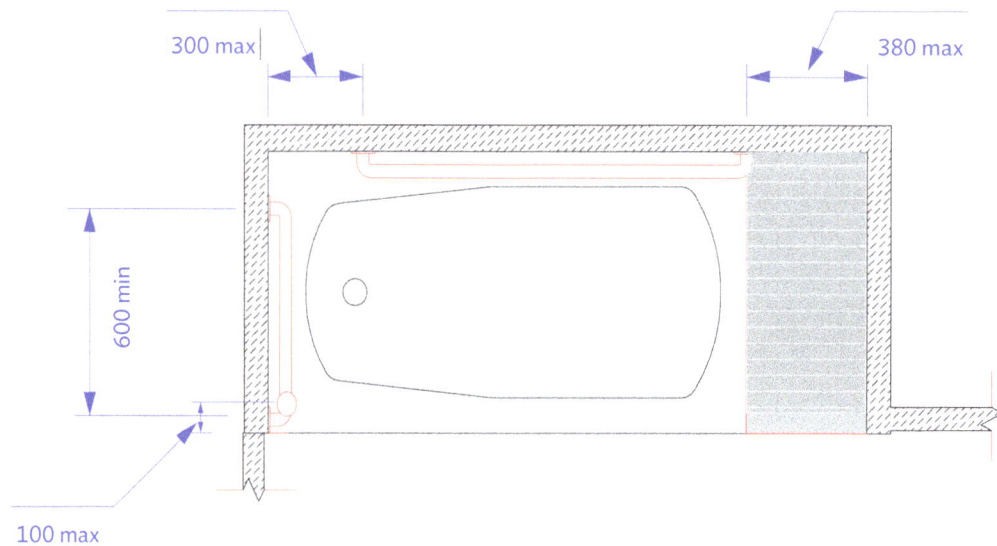

max = maximum, min = minimum.
Source: Government of Georgia. 2020. Resolution 732 on Technical Regulation: National Accessibility Standards. Tbilisi.

Bathtubs with removable seats

- **Back wall.** Two horizontal grab bars must be installed on the back wall at a minimum of 200 mm and a maximum of 250 mm above the rim of the bathtub (Figure 49).
- Each grab bar must be at least 600 mm in length and must be placed at least 600 mm from the head-end wall and extend a maximum of 300 mm from the control-end wall.
- **Head-end wall.** A horizontal grab bar at least 300 mm long must be provided on the head-end wall at the front edge of the bathtub (Figure 50).

Hand shower

- A hand shower must be equipped with a hose at least 1,500 mm long to be used as both a fixed shower head and a hand shower.
- The hand shower must be equipped with a control with a non-positive shut-off feature.
- Where available, an adjustable-height hand shower placed on a vertical bar must be installed in such a way that it does not hamper the use of grab bars.

Bathtub enclosures

- Enclosures for bathtubs must not block access to controls, faucets, and shower and spray units or hamper transfer from wheelchairs onto bathtub seats or into bathtubs.
- Bathtub enclosures must not have tracks placed on the rim of the bathtub.

Figure 49: Grab Bar Requirements for Bathtubs with Removable Seats (Elevation)
(millimeters)

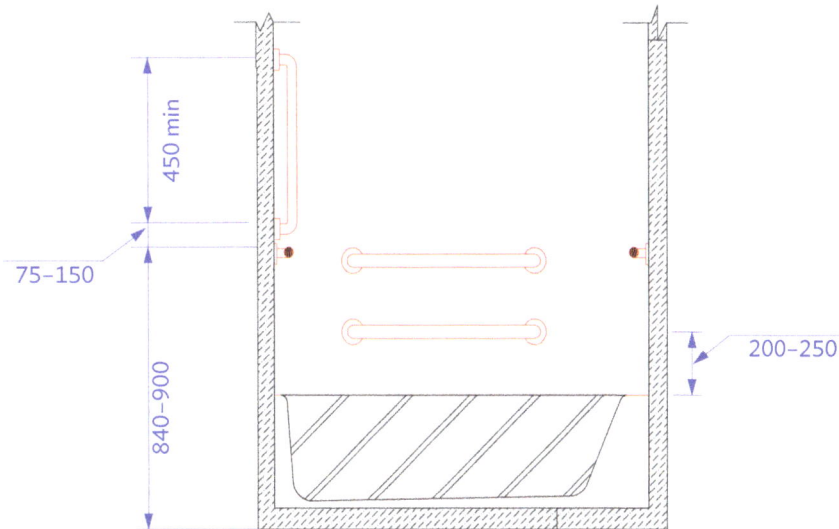

min = minimum.
Source: Government of Georgia. 2020. Resolution 732 on Technical Regulation: National Accessibility Standards. Tbilisi.

Figure 50: Grab Bar Requirements for Bathtubs with Removable Seats (Plan)
(millimeters)

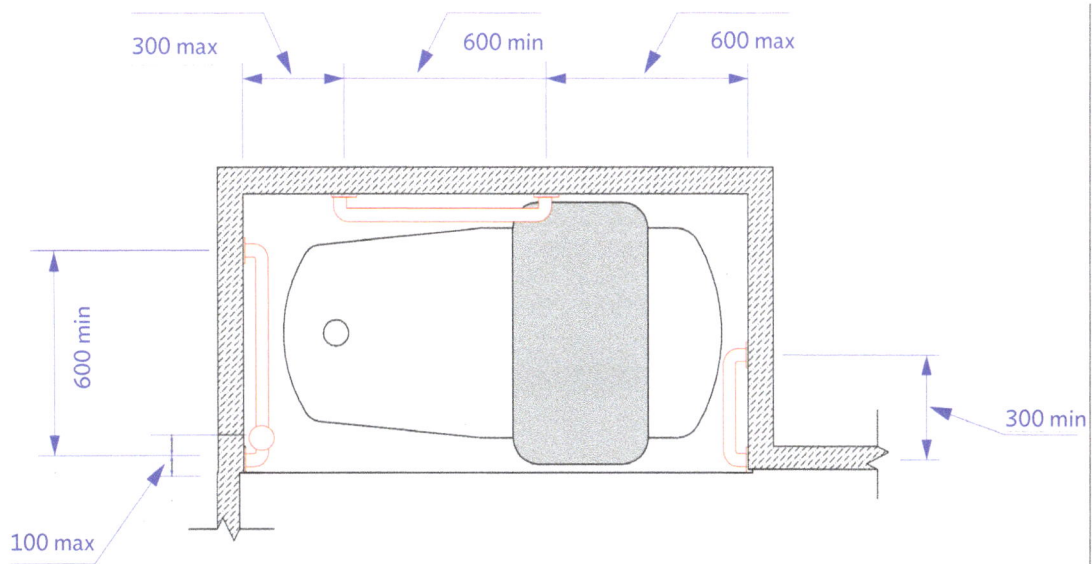

max = maximum, min = minimum.
Source: Government of Georgia. 2020. Resolution 732 on Technical Regulation: National Accessibility Standards. Tbilisi.

Shower Compartments

Transfer-type shower compartments

- **Size.** Transferable shower compartments must have clear inside dimensions of 900 mm wide and 900 mm deep measured at the center point of opposing sides. An entry of at least 900 mm wide must be provided (Figure 51).
- **Clearance.** The clearance provided to open the compartment must be at least 1,300 mm long and 900 mm deep (Figure 52).
- The length of the clear floor space must be measured perpendicular from either the control wall or from 100 mm behind the control wall (Figure 52).
- **Horizontal grab bars.** Horizontal grab bars must be placed both across the control wall and on the back wall at 450 mm from the control wall.
- **Vertical grab bar.** A vertical grab bar at least 450 mm long must be placed on the control-end wall at a minimum of 75 mm and a maximum of 150 mm above the horizontal grab bar, and a maximum of 100 mm inward from the front edge of the shower.

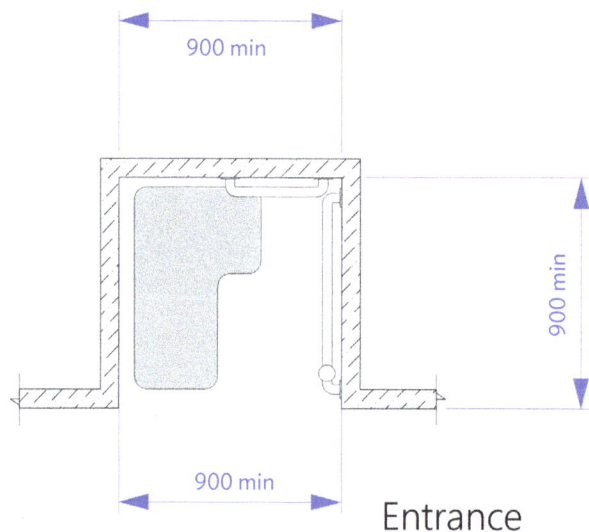

Figure 51: Transfer-Type Shower Compartment Specifications
(millimeters)

900 min

900 min

900 min

Entrance

min = minimum.
Source: Government of Georgia. 2020. Resolution 732 on Technical Regulation: National Accessibility Standards. Tbilisi.

Standard roll-in-type shower compartments

- **Size.** Standard compartments for roll-in type showers must have clear inside dimensions of at least 1,500 mm in width and 760 mm in depth measured at the center point of opposing sides. There must have an entry at least 1,500 mm wide (Figure 53).
- **Clearance.** A clearance of at least 1,500 mm in length must be provided adjacent to an open face shower compartment that is 1,500 mm wide and 760 mm deep (Figure 54).

Figure 52: Transfer-Type Shower Compartments Clearance
(millimeters)

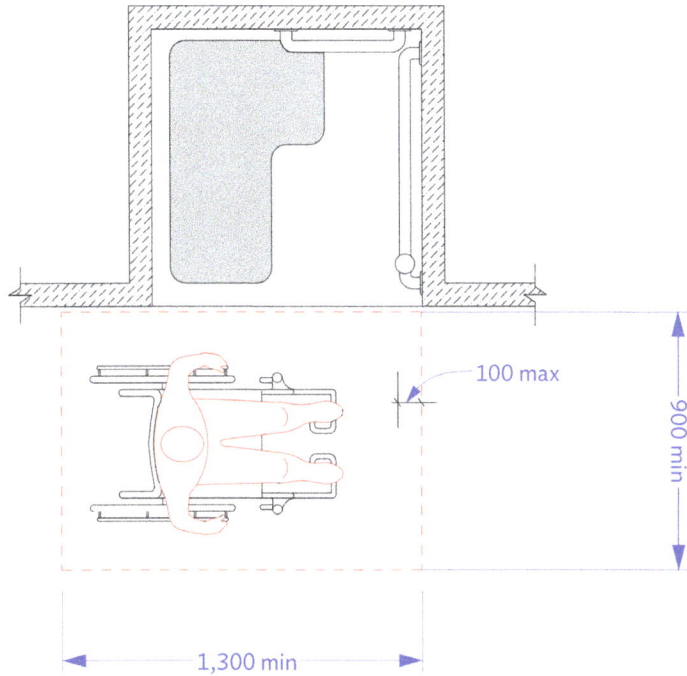

100 max

900 min

1,300 min

max = maximum, min = minimum.
Source: Government of Georgia. 2020. Resolution 732 on Technical Regulation: National Accessibility Standards. Tbilisi.

Figure 53: Standard Roll-in-Type Shower Compartments
(millimeters)

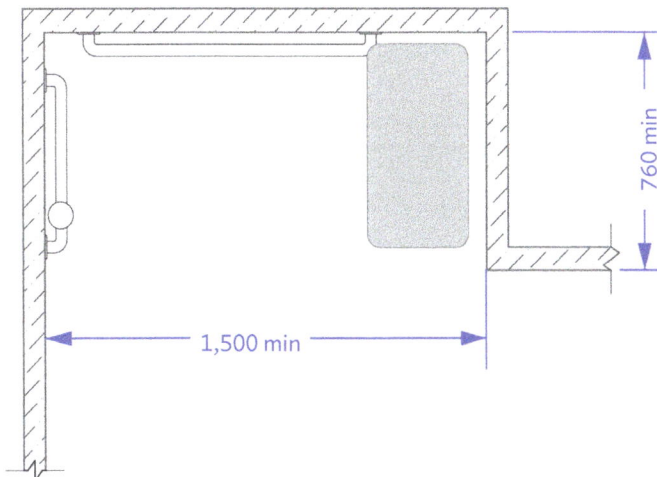

760 min

1,500 min

min = minimum.
Source: Government of Georgia. 2020. Resolution 732 on Technical Regulation: National Accessibility Standards. Tbilisi.

Figure 54: Standard Roll-in-Type Shower Compartments Clearance
(millimeters)

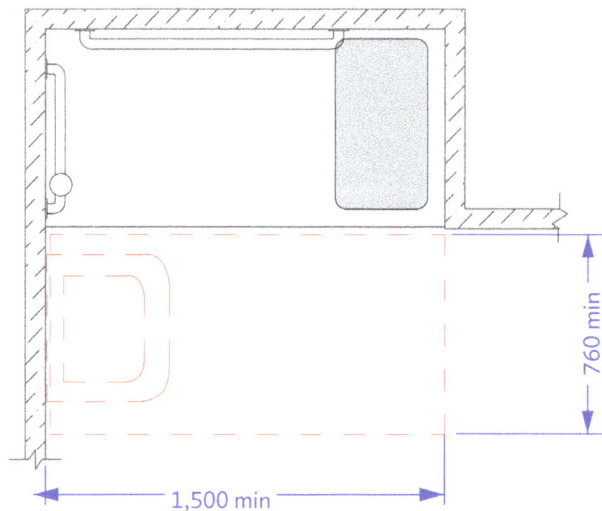

760 min

1,500 min

min = minimum.
Source: Government of Georgia. 2020. Resolution 732 on Technical Regulation: National Accessibility Standards. Tbilisi.

Alternate roll-in-type shower compartments

- **Size.** Compartments with an alternate roll-in shower must have clear inside dimensions of at least 1,500 mm wide and 900 mm deep measured at the center point of opposing sides. An entry at least 900 mm wide must be provided at one end of a 1,500 mm wide compartment. A seat with a minimum length of 600 mm and a maximum length of 900 mm must be placed on the entry side of the compartment (Figure 55).

Figure 55: Alternate Roll-in Shower Compartments
(millimeters)

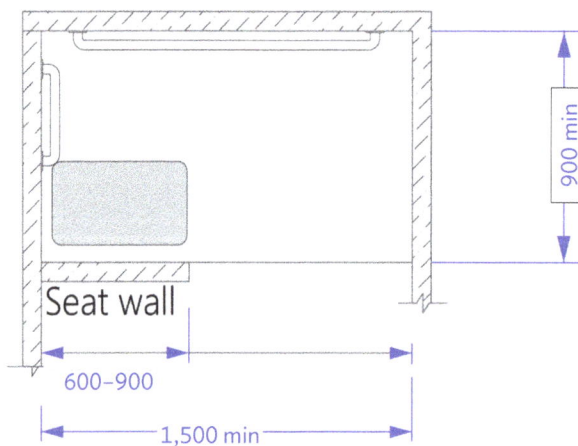

900 min

Seat wall

600–900

1,500 min

min = minimum.
Source: Government of Georgia. 2020. Resolution 732 on Technical Regulation: National Accessibility Standards. Tbilisi.

Grab Bars

Transfer-type shower grab bars

- **Horizontal grab bars.** Horizontal grab bars must be placed across the control wall and on the back wall at 450 mm from the control wall (Figure 56).
- **Vertical grab bar.** A vertical grab bar at least 450 mm long must be placed on the control wall at a minimum of 75 mm and a maximum of 150 mm from the horizontal grab bar, and a maximum of 100 mm inward from the front edge of the shower.

Figure 56: Transfer-Type Shower Grab Bar Specifications
(millimeters)

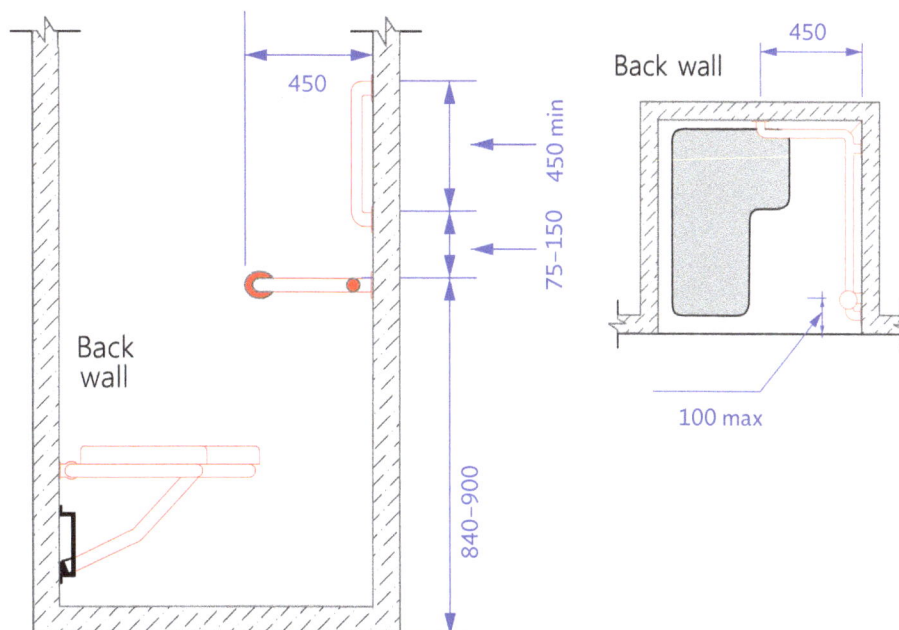

max = maximum, min = minimum.
Source: Government of Georgia. 2020. Resolution 732 on Technical Regulation: National Accessibility Standards. Tbilisi.

Standard roll-in-type shower grab bars

- **Back-wall grab bar.** A grab bar must be placed on the back wall. It should begin at the edge of the seat, not above the seat. The grab bar must extend the length of the wall within 150 mm maximum from the sidewall adjacent to the seat.
- **Sidewall grab bars.** If a sidewall stands across the seat within 1,800 mm of the seat wall, a grab bar must be installed on the side wall across the seat. The sidewall grab bar must extend the length of the wall within a maximum of 150 mm from the adjacent back wall.
- **Vertical grab bar.** If a sidewall is located opposite the seat within 1,800 mm of the seat wall, a vertical grab bar must be provided. A vertical grab bar at least 450 mm in length must be made accessible on the end wall at a minimum of 75 mm and a maximum of 150 mm above the horizontal grab bar, and a maximum of 100 mm inward from the front edge of the shower (Figure 57).

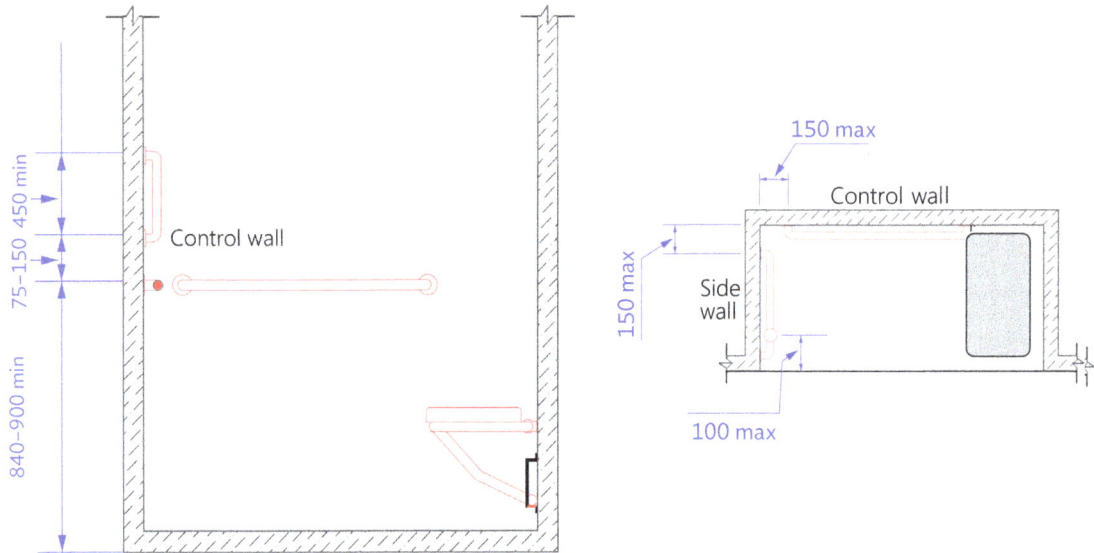

Figure 57: Standard Roll-in-Type Shower Grab Bar Specifications
(millimeters)

max = maximum, min = minimum.
Source: Government of Georgia. 2020. Resolution 732 on Technical Regulation: National Accessibility Standards. Tbilisi.

Alternate roll-in-type shower grab bars

The back wall and sidewall adjacent to the seat must be equipped with grab bars, which must not be provided above the seat. Grab bars must be installed at a maximum of 150 mm from the adjacent wall (Figure 58).

Controls and hand showers

- **In transfer-type showers.** The controls and hand shower must be installed on the control wall across the seat at a minimum of 960 mm and a maximum of 1,200 mm above the shower floor, and at a maximum of 380 mm from the central line of the control wall in the direction of the shower opening.

- **In standard roll-in showers.** The controls and hand shower must be located above the seat. They must be installed on the back wall, at a minimum of 960 mm and a maximum of 1,200 mm above the shower floor, and a minimum of 400 mm and a maximum of 680 mm from the wall behind the seat.

- **In alternate roll-in showers.** The controls and hand shower must be located a minimum of 960 mm and a maximum of 1,200 mm above the shower floor.

- If the controls and hand shower are installed on the end wall adjacent to the seat, the control and hand shower must be located a minimum of 400 mm and a maximum of 680 mm from the wall behind the seat wall.

- If the controls and hand shower are installed on the back wall across the seat, the controls and hand shower should be installed within a maximum of 380 mm from the central line of the seat in the direction of the transfer space.

Figure 58: Alternate Roll-in-Type Shower Grab Bars
(millimeters)

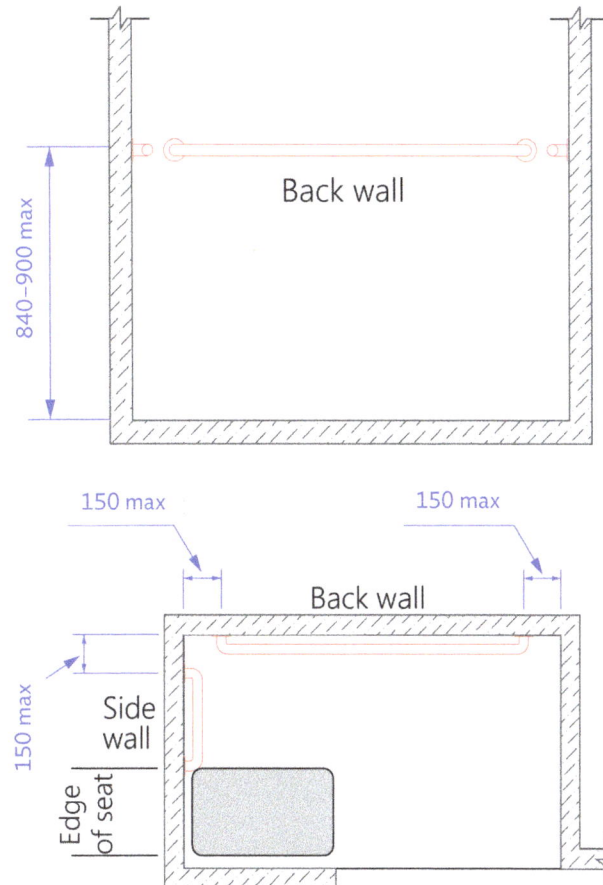

840–900 max

150 max   150 max

Back wall

150 max

Side wall

Edge of seat

max = maximum.
Source: Government of Georgia. 2020. Resolution 732 on Technical Regulation: National Accessibility Standards. Tbilisi.

- **Hand showers.** A hand shower must be equipped with a hose at least 1,500 mm long to be used both as a fixed shower and as a hand shower.
- The hand shower must be equipped with a non-positive, shut-off feature. If provided, an adjustable-height hand shower placed on a vertical bar shall be installed in such a way as not to hamper the use of grab bars.
- An instrument to hold the hand shower wand in the on or off position must be installed at a minimum of 960 mm and a maximum of 1,200 mm above the shower floor.
- **Thresholds.** The height of roll-in-type shower compartment thresholds must not exceed 13 mm.
- In transfer-type shower compartments, with thresholds of up to 13 mm in height, must be beveled, rounded, or vertical.
- **Shower enclosures.** Enclosures for shower compartments must be built so as not to block access to controls or obstruct transfer from wheelchairs onto shower seats.

Seats

Bathtub seats

- Bathtub seats must be located a minimum of 430 mm and a maximum of 485 mm above the bathroom floor, measured to the top of the seat.
- Removable in-tub seats, which are designed to ensure secure placement, must be a minimum of 380 mm and a maximum of 400 mm deep.
- Permanent seats must be no less than 380 mm in depth and extend from the back wall to or beyond the outer edge of the bathtub. Seats must be located at the head end of the bathtub.

Shower compartment seats

- The minimum height for a shower compartment seat is 430 mm with the maximum being 485 mm measured from the bathroom floor to the top of the seat.
- In compartments with transfer-type and alternate roll-in-type showers, the seat must extend along the seat wall within 75 mm of the compartment entry.
- In standard roll-in-type showers, the seat must extend from the control wall to a point within 75 mm of the compartment entry.

Rectangular shower seats

- The rear edge of a rectangular seat must be a maximum of 65 mm from the seat wall; the front edge must be a minimum of 380 mm and a maximum of 400 mm from the seat wall (Figure 59).

Figure 59: Specifications for Rectangular Shower Seats
(millimeters)

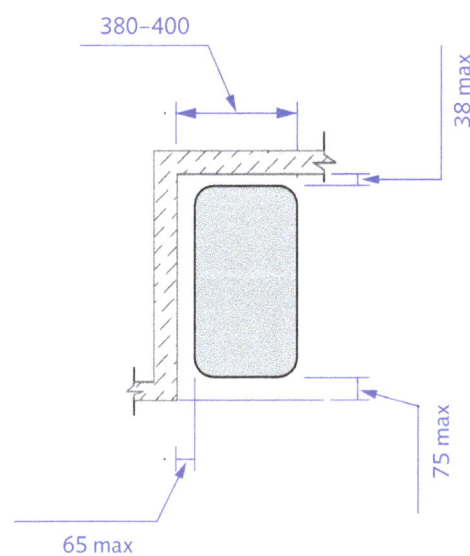

380–400

38 max

75 max

65 max

max = maximum.

Source: Government of Georgia. 2020. Resolution 732 on Technical Regulation: National Accessibility Standards. Tbilisi.

- The distance between the side edge of the seat and the back wall of a transfer-type shower should not exceed 40 mm. The same distance must be ensured between the side edge of the seat and the control wall of a roll-in-type shower.

Shaped seats

- The rear edge of an L-shaped seat must be a maximum of 65 mm from the seat wall, and the front edge must be a minimum of 380 mm and a maximum of 400 mm from the seat wall (Figure 60).
- The rear edge of the "L" portion of the seat must not exceed 40 mm from the wall. The front edge must be a minimum of 350 mm and a maximum of 380 mm from the wall.
- The end of the "L" must be a minimum of 560 mm and a maximum of 580 mm from the main seat wall.

Grab bars in toilet or bathing facilities must comply with the following specifications:

- **Circular cross section.** Grab bars with a circular cross section must have an outside diameter of at least 30 mm and a maximum of 50 mm.
- **Noncircular cross section.** Grab bars with a noncircular cross section must have a maximum cross section dimension of 50 mm and a perimeter dimension of at least 100 mm and not more than 120 mm.

Figure 60: Specifications for Shaped Shower Seats
(millimeters)

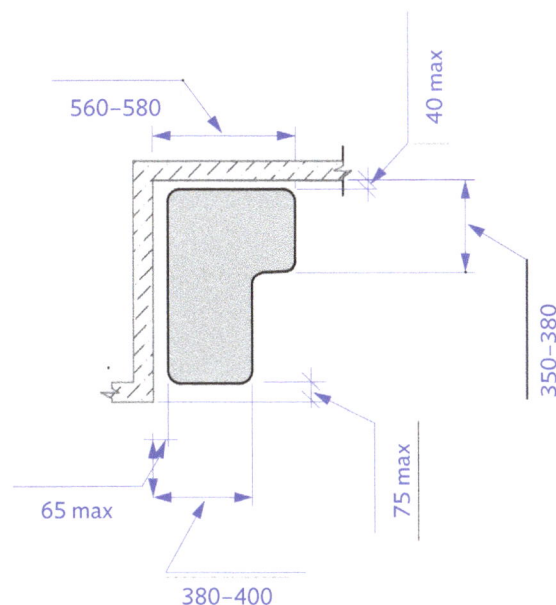

max = maximum.
Source: Government of Georgia. 2020. Resolution 732 on Technical Regulation: National Accessibility Standards. Tbilisi.

- **Spacing.** The space between the wall and the grab bar must be 40 mm. The space between the grab bar and projecting objects below and at the ends of the grab bar must be at least 40 mm. The space between the grab bar and projecting objects above the grab bar must be at least 300 mm.

- **Position.** Grab bars must be installed in a horizontal position at least 840 mm and a maximum of 900 mm above the floor measured to the top of the gripping surface.

- **Surface hazards.** Grab bars and any wall or other surfaces adjacent to them must be free of sharp or abrasive objects. Edges must be rounded, and grab bars must not rotate within their fittings.

- **Installation and configuration.** Grab bars shall be installed in a way that provides a gripping surface at the locations specified in this standard and does not obstruct the clear floor space. Horizontal and vertical grab bars must be allowed to be separate bars, a single piece bar, or combination thereof.

Assembly Areas

Wheelchair spaces

- **Slope and dimensions.** The floor surface of wheelchair space locations must have a slope not steeper than 1:48.

- A single wheelchair space must be 900 mm wide (Figure 61). If two adjacent wheelchair spaces are provided, each must be at least 840 mm wide (Figure 62).

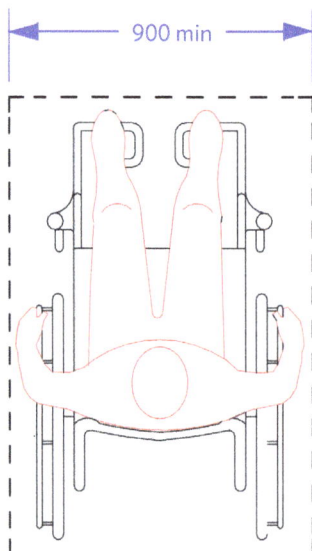

Figure 61: Single Wheelchair Space
(millimeters)

900 min

min = minimum.
Source: Government of Georgia. 2020. Resolution 732 on Technical Regulation: National Accessibility Standards. Tbilisi.

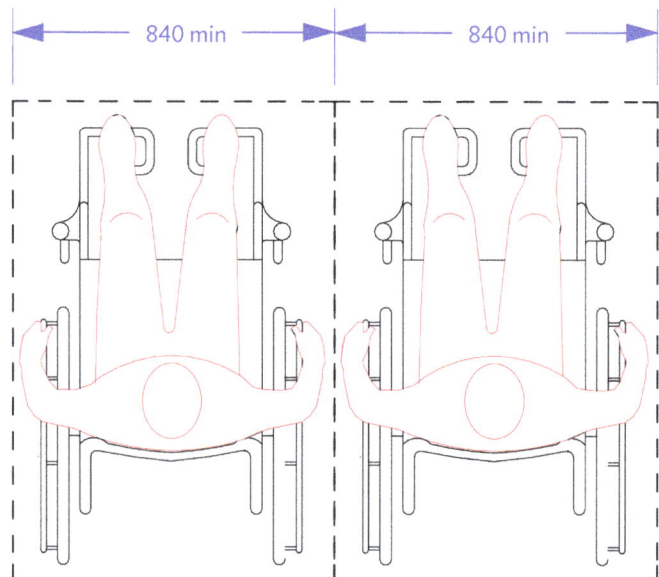

Figure 62: Two Adjacent Wheelchair Space
(millimeters)

840 min   840 min

min = minimum.
Source: Government of Georgia. 2020. Resolution 732 on Technical Regulation: National Accessibility Standards. Tbilisi.

- If a wheelchair space has an opening from the front or rear, the wheelchair space must be at least 1,300 mm deep (Figure 63).
- If a wheelchair space is only open from the side, it must be at least 1,500 mm deep (Figure 64).

Figure 63: Depth of Wheelchair Space in Area Front or Rear Access
(millimeters)

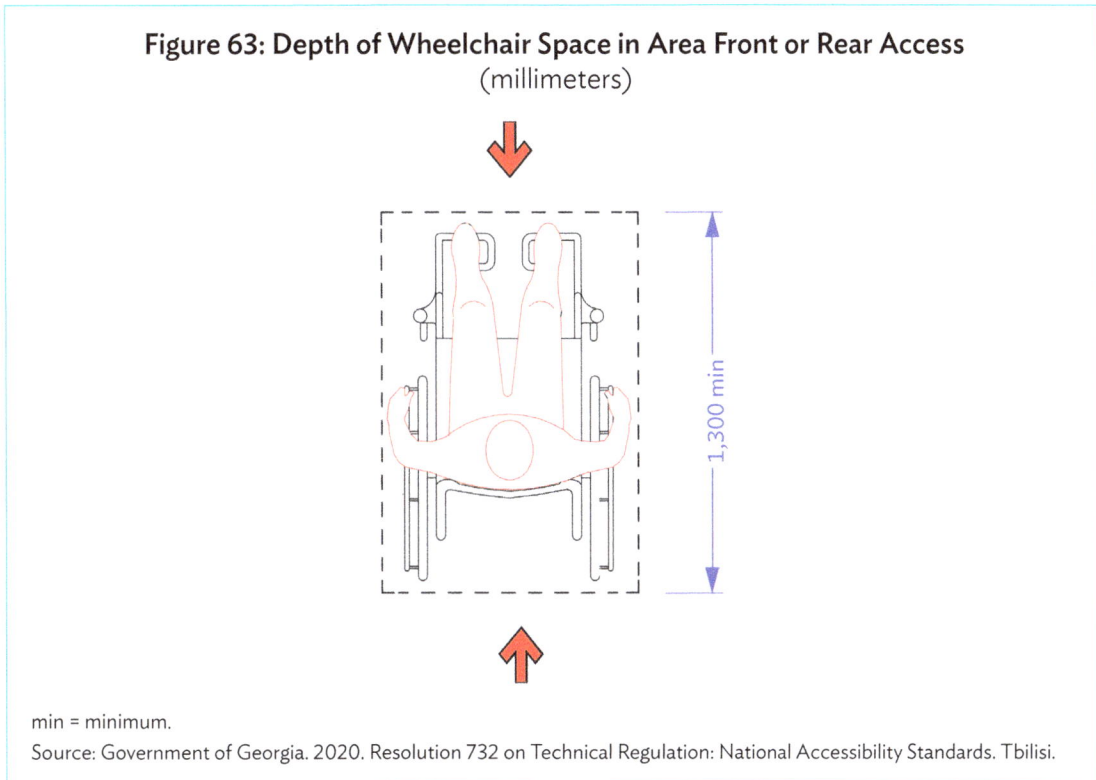

min = minimum.
Source: Government of Georgia. 2020. Resolution 732 on Technical Regulation: National Accessibility Standards. Tbilisi.

Figure 64: Wheelchair Space with Opening to the Side
(millimeters)

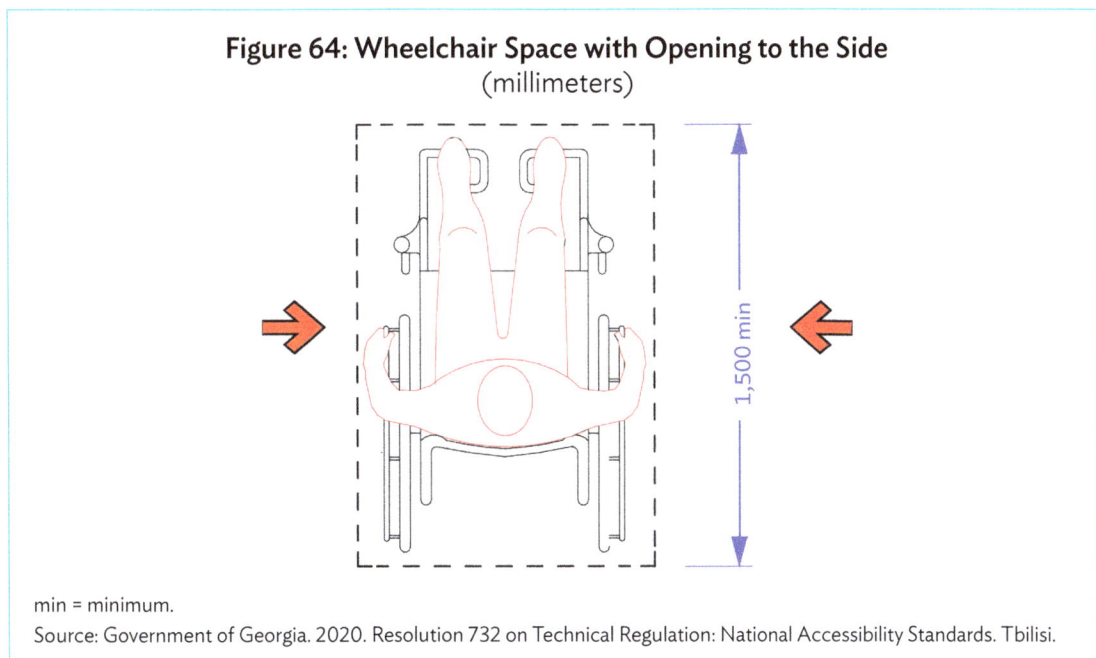

min = minimum.
Source: Government of Georgia. 2020. Resolution 732 on Technical Regulation: National Accessibility Standards. Tbilisi.

Wheelchair space positioning. Wheelchair spaces must adjoin an accessible route that should not overlap with them.

- A wheelchair space must not overlap with the required width of an aisle.
- Wheelchair space locations are to be an integral part of any seating area.
- The shoulder of the wheelchair space occupant should be at least 900 mm from the front and at least 300 mm from the rear of the wheelchair space (Figure 65).

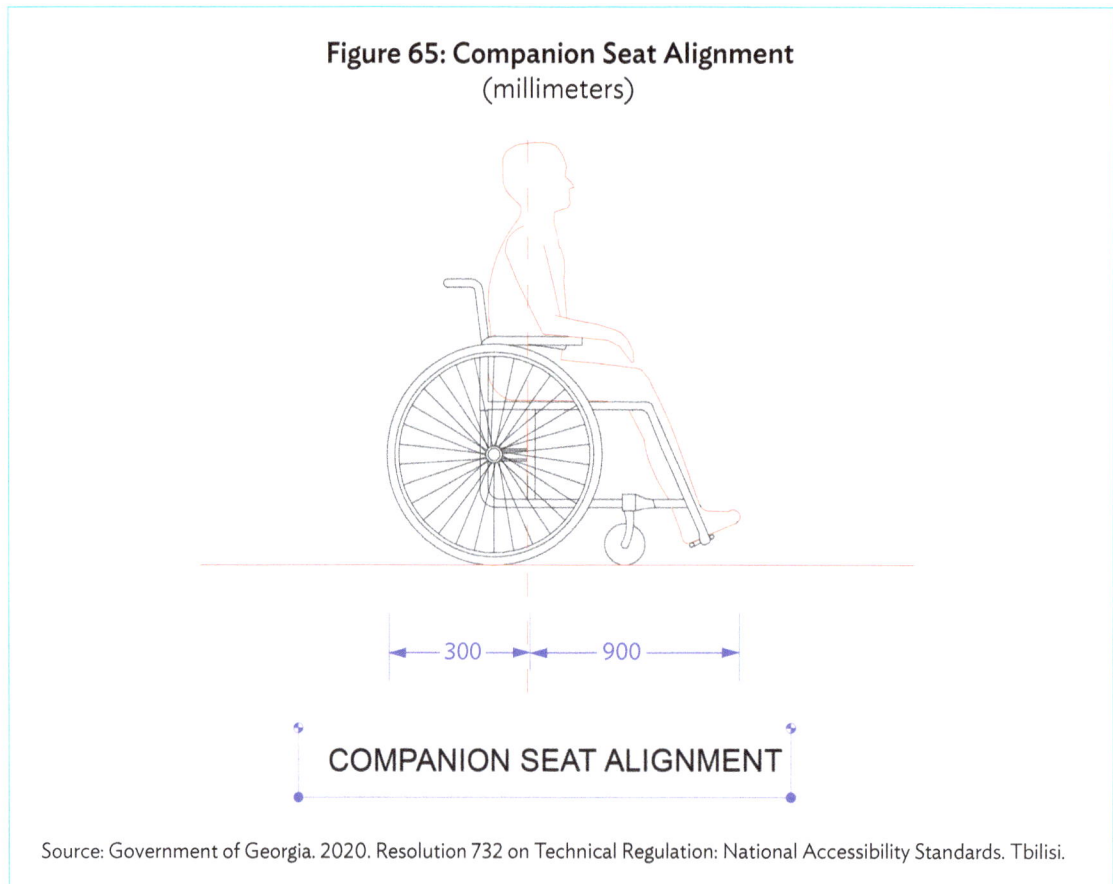

Figure 65: Companion Seat Alignment
(millimeters)

300   900

COMPANION SEAT ALIGNMENT

Source: Government of Georgia. 2020. Resolution 732 on Technical Regulation: National Accessibility Standards. Tbilisi.

Companion seat positioning. The companion seat must be equivalent in size, quality, comfort, and amenities to the seats in the immediate area of the wheelchair space location. Companion seats must be movable.

- In row seating, the companion seat must be located in a way that provides shoulder alignment with the wheelchair space occupant. The floor surface for the companion seat must be of the same elevation as the wheelchair space floor surface.
- Where armrests are provided on seating in the immediate area of designated aisle seats, folding or retractable armrests must be provided on the aisle side of an aisle seat.
- Each designated aisle seat must have an identification sign or a marker.

- **Lines of sight.** Where spectators are expected to remain seated during the events, people seated in a wheelchair space must be provided with lines of sight to the performance area or playing field comparable with that provided to seated spectators in closest proximity to the wheelchair space location.

- Spectators in a wheelchair space must be provided with lines of sight over the heads of seated individuals in the first row in front of the wheelchair space location (Figure 66).

- Spectators in a wheelchair space must be provided with lines of sight over the shoulders and between the heads of seated individuals in the first row in front of the wheelchair space location (Figure 67).

- **Distance from adjacent seating.** The front of the wheelchair space in a wheelchair space location should not exceed 300 mm from the back of the chair or bench in front.

- The height of the floor surface at the wheelchair space location must comply with the dimensions given in Table 3.

- **Horizontal dispersion.** Wheelchair space locations must be distributed horizontally to provide viewing options. If seating encircles the stage or field fully or in part, horizontal distribution must include the entire seating area. Two wheelchair spaces must be permitted to be located side-by-side.

- Wheelchair space locations must be distributed at a variety of distances from the event to ensure access to viewing options.

- Where assembly seating has multiple seating areas with amenities that differ from other distinct seating areas, wheelchair space locations must be ensured within each distinct seating area.

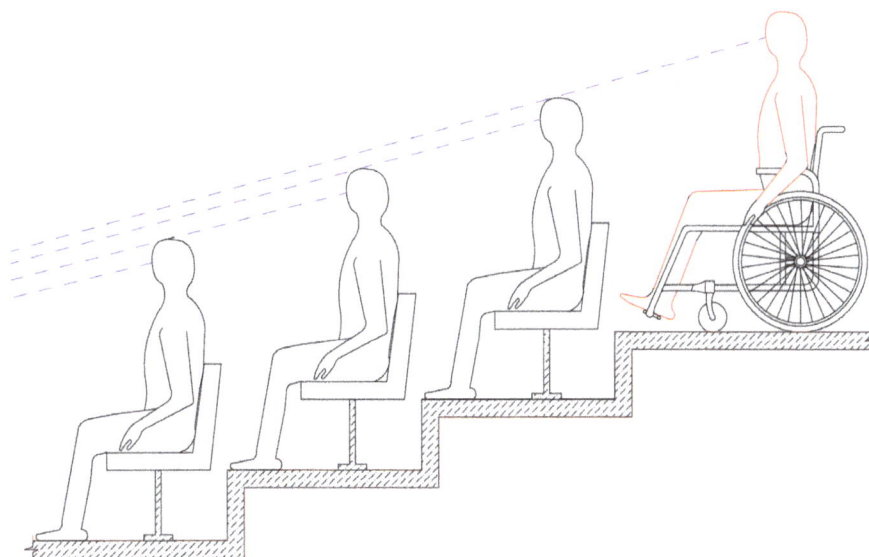

Figure 66: Lines of Sight over Heads

Source: Government of Georgia. 2020. Resolution 732 on Technical Regulation: National Accessibility Standards. Tbilisi.

Figure 67: Lines of Sight between Heads

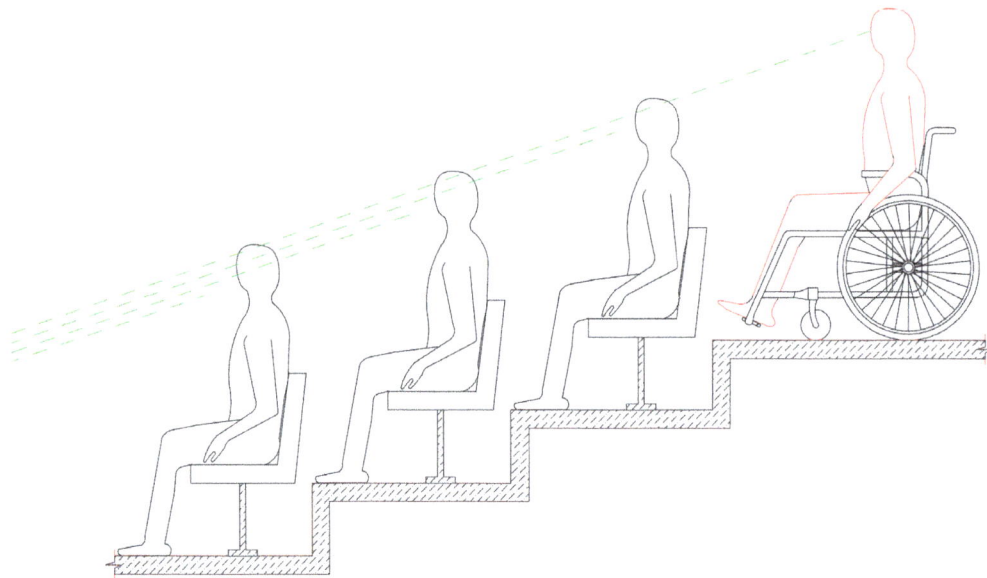

Source: Government of Georgia. 2020. Resolution 732 on Technical Regulation: National Accessibility Standards. Tbilisi.

Table 3: Required Wheelchair Space Location Elevation over Standing Spectators

Riser Height (mm)	Minimum Height of Wheelchair Space Location Based on Row Spacing (mm)		
	Rows less than 840 mm	Rows 840 mm to 1,120 mm	Rows over 1,120 mm
0	405	405	405
100	560	535	535
205	785	760	710
305	1,015	940	890
405	1,245	1,145	1,065
510	1,475	1,345	1,245
610	NA	1,550	1,420
710	NA	1,750	1,600
815	NA	NA	1,955
915 and higher	NA	NA	1,955

mm = millimeter   NA = not applicable.

Source: Government of Georgia. 2020. Resolution 732 on Technical Regulation: National Accessibility Standards. Tbilisi.

Spaces utilized primarily for viewing motion picture projections

- **Spaces with seating on risers.** If seating has a tiered layout, wheelchair space locations must be integrated into the tiered seating area on a riser or a cross-aisle.
- **Distance from the screen.** Wheelchair space locations must be located within the rear 60% of seats provided or within the area of an auditorium in which the vertical viewing angles, as measured to the top of the screen, are from the 40th to the 100th percentile of vertical viewing angles for all seats as ranked from the seats in the first row (1st percentile) to seats in the back row (100th percentile).
- The minimum number of wheelchair space locations must be in accordance with Table 4.

Table 4: Minimum Wheelchair Space Locations

Total Seating in Assembly Areas	Minimum Required Number of Wheelchair Space Locations
Up to 150	1
151 to 500	2
501 to 1,000	3
1,001 to 5,000	3, plus 1 additional space for every 1,000 seats or portions thereof above 1,000
5,001 and over	7, plus 1 additional space for every 2,000 seats or portions thereof above 5,000

Source: Government of Georgia. 2020. Resolution 732 on Technical Regulation: National Accessibility Standards. Tbilisi.

Sign language interpreter stations

- **Area.** A sign language interpreter station must provide a level and clear floor at least 600 mm deep and 900 mm wide that is located to provide a direct line of sight from the seating area.
- **Location.** The sign language interpreter station must be located so that seating within an arc from the station measured to the left and to the right 60 degrees within 20.0 m horizontal distance from the station is provided with sight lines that give a view of the sign language station from a height of 900 mm to 1,800 mm above the floor of the station.
- **Illumination.** The sign language interpreter station must be equipped with lighting facilities capable of providing 110 lux of illuminance while signing is underway measured at the center of the floor of the sign language station at a height of 1,200 mm above the floor.
- **Backdrop.** If a sign language interpreter station is located with a permanent wall less than 3,000 mm behind the sign language interpreter station, the permanent wall to a height of 2,500 mm from the finish floor must be considered as a backdrop that should provide a flat, smooth surface with a monochromatic, low-luster finish treatment.

Case Study: Assembly Areas

Wheelchair user viewing positions are important to ensure that wheelchair users have a good experience of the venue and performance or activity being watched. They should be integrated into surrounding seating to provide an equitable crowd experience while also offering excellent views of the performance area at all times, including when spectators in the row in front stand up.

Photos by Iain McKinnon.

Lighting

Lighting is not only functional, but also a design element of indoor and outdoor environments. It can be used to illuminate directional paths, entry points, keypads, and informational signs. The use of multiple light sources with different types of lighting is important for safety, security, and comfort for everyone, and, in particular, people with a visual impairment.

Appropriately placed light sources help people with visual impairments to easily navigate within the environment. People with hearing impairments also benefit from the proper use of lighting in the environment in addition to serving as alerts for safety reasons.

Ambient lighting. Ambient lighting in outdoor and indoor spaces helps create and add to the feeling of a space. These lights can have dimmers, timers, and motion detectors added to make a space more functional. Ambient light should not be too bright or cause glare and should be accompanied by other light sources to reduce shadows.

Task lighting. Task lighting highlights an area or workspace to complement the ambient light. Good task lighting helps reduce shadows and glare and can help reduce eyestrain.

Accent lighting. Accent lighting draws attention to, and can help make people aware of, a hazard, such as the edge of a train platform. The purpose of accent lighting is to draw attention to the item or situation that needs to be seen rather than the light itself.

Natural lighting. Natural light is an important component of any lighting arrangement and can create an ambience of its own. The effect of the natural light on a space changes according to the direction of the sun and the different seasons.

Universal Design for Neurodiversity

Neurodiversity is a relatively new term that recognizes the diversity of human cognition and includes people with autism, dyslexia, dementia, and other cognitive impairments.

Universal design of the physical environment and surroundings has an important role to play in supporting neurodivergent people. In most cases, the focus is on sensory information and minimizing the negative impact some physical environments can have. Therefore, there is a strong emphasis on lighting, surface finishes, acoustics, olfactory clues (smell), and touch. Some people also need the option to have space and quieter places to go and there is also a consideration for building management.

Lighting and window treatments. Some neurodiverse people can find harsh lighting uncomfortable and distracting. Therefore, soft, adjustable lighting is preferred, especially in living and educational settings. The same caution should be considered when selecting blinds and curtains. Blackout blinds or curtains should be provided in spaces where harsh daylight or glare is problematic and when periods of no light are likely to be beneficial.

Colors and surface finishes. Colors play an important role in creating a friendly and supportive environment for neurodivergent people. Multicolor and/or patterned surface finishes can be confusing and anxiety-inducing for some people. Therefore, simple designs and colors are preferred for walls and floors. Providing clear, simple contrasts between key surfaces such as floors, walls, and door frames can support all building users and some neurodivergent people.

Acoustics and noise. For many people, including neurodivergent people, excessive noise can be distracting and uncomfortable. Careful consideration of the acoustic quality and treatment of the built environment is particularly important to reduce excessive noise. Soft carpeting or flooring is one way to help reduce and minimize excessive noise and create a more comfortable atmosphere. Acoustic baffling treatments can also be used to reduce reverberation times and help reduce the level of background noise.

Olfactory and touch. For some people, certain smells and/or textures have the potential to cause anxiety or even physical pain. Therefore, it is important to consider these factors in the design of the built environment to ensure any such "triggers" are designed out as far as it is possible to do so. Consideration should be given to good extraction and ventilation where food is being cooked to prevent excessive smells and aromas. Another consideration can also be to use natural and warm materials where possible. The key here will be to consult with the building operators and local users to ascertain any specific sensory issues that need to be considered in advance taking into account the local contexts.

Building management and quiet spaces. The way a public facility is managed also plays a significant role in how supportive and accessible it is for neurodivergent people. Avoiding unnecessary crowding, allowing fast track queuing, and providing quiet spaces for people to take a break from busy public spaces can greatly improve someone's experience and even make the difference in their ability to visit or not.

Case Study: Universal Design for Neurodiversity

It is important to consider a diverse range of disabled people, including neurodiverse people. Some examples that support neurodiverse people include pods that offer an enclosed workspace in an open plan office and the provision of multi-sensory room at airports to support people, including autistic people, who benefit from this facility when travelling.

Photo by ie-uk.com.

Photo by Gatwick Airport.

Key Recommendations for Web Accessibility

Access to information via digital means is important for all citizens, including people with disabilities. Blind people can use websites if they are correctly coded and designed to be readable by screen readers, which can read a page aloud to the user. The globally accepted standard for accessible webpages and digital communications is given in the World Wide Web Consortium Web Content Accessibility Guidelines.[67] All public service websites, mobile apps, digital "kiosks," and other digital services should be designed according to these guidelines. Translations of the guidelines are available, but there is no Georgian language version.[68] Some of the key features of accessible websites are as follows:

Background color changer. By clicking the drop-down button, a user can change the background color to the desired one (i.e., white, black, dark blue, gray, brown). If wanted, a new color can be added.

---

[67]   W3C (World Wide Web Consortium) Web Accessibility Initiative. Web Content Accessibility Guidelines (WCAG) Overview. https://www.w3.org/WAI/standards-guidelines/wcag/.

[68]   W3C Web Accessibility Initiative. WCAG 2 Translations. https://www.w3.org/WAI/standards-guidelines/wcag/translations/.

Text color changer. By clicking the drop-down button, a user can change the color of any text displayed on a webpage.

Resizing. Users can easily resize a webpage, making it bigger or smaller. The system remembers a command and retains it until another command is given.

Audio button. The audio button enables blind people to listen to any information displayed on a webpage.

Alternative text for images and animations. Using the alt attribute provides descriptions of visual content to support visually impaired users.[69]

---

[69] Web Content Accessibility Guidelines (WCAG) 2.1. https://www.w3.org/TR/WCAG/.

CASE STUDIES AND EXAMPLES

Accessible Tourism Examples: Cities and Destinations

Recognizing the competitive advantage of accessibility, a growing number of cities and destinations around the world have made great efforts to establish themselves as accessible tourist destinations, delivering good access and inclusion for their own citizens with disabilities and to tourists of all ages and abilities. In particular, many European cities are working to build their reputations as accessible, livable cities that offer a warm welcome to all visitors. Boxes 1 to 3 present good examples of inclusive urban development in London, Barcelona, and Tokyo.

Box 1: Queen Elizabeth Olympic Park, London

The Queen Elizabeth Olympic Park (QEOP) in London is considered a good example of inclusive urban development. Building on the Paralympic legacy of the London 2012 Games, the subsequent development on and around QEOP sets a high benchmark for inclusive design.

There was a clear process in place to deliver inclusive design. This ensured that inclusive design was considered from the very beginning of any project and throughout. Persons with disabilities were involved in the design and development process, helping ensure that outcomes considered the widest possible range of user needs.

This process resulted in inclusive buildings (public and residential), inclusive public realm, and inclusive services that supported all members of the community, local and international.

The demographic of the local population was considered in the design and development of the Queen Elizabeth Olympic Park and its venues. With London as one of the most diverse areas in the United Kingdom, there is a high proportion of people of Muslim faith living around the park. As such, facilities including multifaith rooms were provided where people could go for prayer. Toilet and changing facilities were also designed considering the need for ablutions, and to avoid aligning with Mecca.

continued on next page

Box 1 *continued*

Level changes exist across the site. Care was taken to ensure that a choice of access routes was provided, including mechanical and nonmechanical solutions. Sloped routes are provided with gradients made as shallow as possible. These routes are complemented with external passenger lifts, located adjacent to the stairs. This provides solutions that support all potential users.

There was an aspiration for the park to minimize the use of private vehicles and instead promote use of public transport. This was for sustainability reasons and also to promote the excellent public transport infrastructure available. However, accessible parking spaces have still been provided at all park venues to support persons with disabilities for whom their own private vehicle may be their only option to travel.

Photos by GDI Hub/London Legacy Development Corporation.
Source: Global Disability Innovation Hub. Inclusive Design Standards updated for 2019.

Box 2: Accessible Tourism, Barcelona

Barcelona is working hard to achieve inclusion for persons with disabilities (residents and visitors) to help create a cohesive city that supports quality of life for everyone and respect for diversity. This includes ensuring that the facilities of the most popular places or attractions and the public transport systems are inclusive and accessible.

The Barcelona Accessible Tourism website has been created as tool for visitors and residents alike. It provides a wealth of information and offers examples of the kind of work being done, including museums that support people that are blind and partially sighted, hotels with inclusive facilities and rooms, beaches that offer accessible facilities, and sign-language tours of the city.

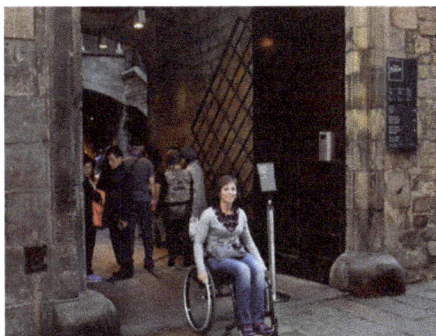

The Museu Picasso is listed on the Barcelona Accessible Tourism website as an inclusive attraction where visitors with disabilities are welcome. This will help increase the number of visitors in general.

Some of the museum's key inclusive features include multilanguage audio guide, group tours for visitors with a hearing impairment, priority queuing for people with mobility impairments, passenger lifts accessible around the building, and wheelchairs available to loan on request.

continued on next page

Box 2 *continued*

Like many developed cities, Barcelona's metro system was built around a century ago and at a time when inclusive design was not a consideration. However, all new stations built, and stations renovated since 1992 (when the city was a Paralympic Games host) are accessible. Some features include barriers with acoustic and visual signals, platform screen doors, and audio ticket machines to help people with a visual impairment.

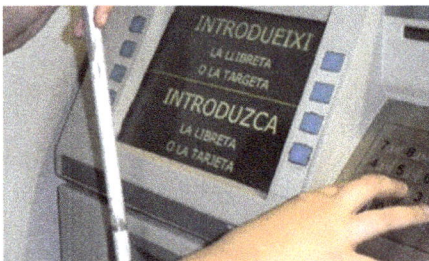

CaixaBank ATMs are accessible for people with a visual impairment, providing audio information in a secure way. Most of the bank's branches are also accessible providing level access and counters at heights to accommodate people in both a seated and standing position. The bank's website provides customers with details about what branches offer what accessible features, thus empowering the customer.

Photos by Barcelona Turisme.
Source: Barcelona Accessible Tourism. http://www.barcelona-access.com.

Box 3: Universal Design, Tokyo

The city of Tokyo is considered a strong advocate for applying universal design. This is evident in a number of different ways around the city.

However, for some, there remains a need for better "inclusive design" solutions that consider an even greater diversity of end user and that are co-developed with persons with disabilities rather than being provided for them without proper consultation.

In preparation for the 2020 Paralympic Games, Tokyo was particularly engaged in ensuring that the city was ready for a large number of visitors with disabilities. The examples below demonstrate how the city accommodated its visitors that have additional support needs.

Tactile guidance paving is used around the city along main circulation routes, on pavements and leading to and from main transport stations. These are intended primarily to support people with a visual impairment.

It is important that tactile guidance paving is applied in a considered and consistent way to be genuinely effective. Too much can be confusing, disorienting, and even present an access barrier to mobility aid.

continued on next page

Box 3 *continued*

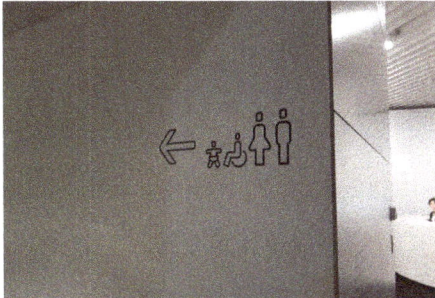

Signage and use of pictograms are often well considered, particularly within public buildings. It is expected that this reflects a country with a large proportion of international visitors who benefit from symbols and pictograms when Japanese is not their first language.

This also supports many neurodiverse people who find symbols and pictograms easier to process and understand than text only. Text is also important in addition to graphics.

Braille indication and visual warnings were observed on handrails to stairs.

These support people with a visual impairment when using stairs and handrails by providing a tactile warning message that the stairs are about to end. This helps prevent trips and falls that are common as people transfer between stairs and level landings.

Photos by Iain McKinnon.
Source : Go Tokyo. Accessibility. https://www.gotokyo.org/en/plan/accessibility/index.html.

European Capital of Smart Tourism Award

This European Commission initiative was launched in 2018. The European Capital of Smart Tourism award recognizes outstanding achievements in smart tourism in European cities. Smart tourism responds to new challenges and demands in a fast-changing sector, including the evolution of digital tools, products, and services; equal opportunity and access for all visitors; sustainable development of the local area; and support to creative industries, local talent, and heritage.

For this initiative, the cornerstones of smart tourism are defined as excellence in four award categories:

(i)   Accessibility
(ii) Sustainability
(iii) Digitalization
(iv) Cultural heritage and creativity

For more examples, a detailed description of each category, and additional information, refer to the *Guide for Applicants*.[70]

[70]   European Capital of Smart Tourism. 2019. *Guide for Applicants*. http://smarttourismcapital.eu/downloads/guide-for-applicants.pdf.

More than 30 candidate cities submitted portfolios for the award. The overall winners of the 2019 award were Helsinki, Finland; and Lyon, France. Both winners have made long-term efforts to create smart environments for tourists in their cities. Four additional cities were recognized with European Smart Tourism awards for sustainability (Ljubljana, Slovenia), accessibility (Malaga, Spain), digitalization (Copenhagen, Denmark), and cultural heritage and creativity (Linz, Austria).

Helsinki prepared a draft program of activities for 2019 to cement its position as a leader in smart tourism. The following is a short extract of their planning document, where they focus on accessibility and information as key factors in developing the tourism of the future.

> For us, smart is more than just a buzzword. Our aim is to become the most functional city in the world for everyone—for locals and visitors alike. Our developing city is digitally savvy enough to unite players. We aim to be accessible and agile. That is why we can adapt to multiple needs and transform if that is what is needed. We are stylish and creative, and we have a team mentality: we do things together. Nothing happens in Helsinki without citizen involvement. As stated in the Helsinki city strategy, we are committed to maintaining an ongoing dialogue with the local community about the impacts of growing tourism. Our smartness is our source of pride, and the title of European Capital of Smart Tourism would help us gather stakeholders under one umbrella and define a raison d'etre for our efforts.
>
> Our tourism road map is ambitious. For example, we aim to completely change how we collect, catalogue, and share tourism information. Instead of measuring the basics, we are teaming up with players to harness tourism data into a powerful tool to make our tourism thrive. And it is not just business that we will measure. We are looking into new ways of measuring tourism's impact on the environment and its overall sustainability. We want to take the guesswork out of the tourism business. This would function as one of our key initiatives of the title year.[71]

European Commission Access City Awards

The European Commission Access City Award was established in 2010 to promote accessibility in European cities and make Europe an easy place to live for everyone, especially for persons with disabilities and the elderly.[72] The award provides a platform for sharing best practice on accessibility of the environment and building infrastructure. Through this platform, the European Commission supports cities in striving to ensure accessibility for all.

The Access City Award forms part of the European Union (EU) Disability Strategy 2010–2020. It recognizes cities that have demonstrated clear and sustainable developments to improve urban accessibility. Candidates must have more than 50,000 inhabitants and show improvements in (i) the built environment and public spaces, (ii) transport and infrastructure, (iii) information and communication technology and new technologies, and (iv) public facilities and services. Boxes 4 to 8 present the good practices of previous Access City Award winners.

---

[71]   Initiative of the European Union. *Helsinki: Taking Smart to New Heights*. https://tinyurl.com/ycztuper.

[72]   European Commission. Access City Award. https://ec.europa.eu/social/main.jsp?catId=1141.

Box 4: Jönköping, Sweden—2021 Access City Award Winner

Jönköping, in the south of Sweden, made continuous improvements in both the new and old areas of the city, in collaboration with disability organizations.

The city also created a local Access City Award for businesses or organizations that worked with their customers to improve accessibility.

The library and concert hall now include tactile maps and signage, audio description, easy to read facilities, and level access. A total of 120 public playgrounds have been renovated to improve accessibility for children with disabilities.

Tactile maps and signages as well as street-level accessibility features found in Jonkoping.
Source: European Commission Access City Awards.

Box 5: Warsaw, Poland—2020 Access City Award Winner

Pathways, bicycle lanes, and pavements across the city have been upgraded to be more accessible. Roads, public spaces, and building renovations must now comply with accessibility regulations.

All 30 metro stations have been upgraded to improve access, and all buses and 87 bus stops have been renovated to meet the accessibility standards.

The city is also developing accessibility requirements for its website and nearly 300 employees have been trained on the use of these. Accessible mobile applications are also being developed, and the city plans to invest more in digital communication in the future.

Accessibility ramps for public transport, playgrounds and open spaces in Warsaw.
Source: European Commission Access City Awards.

Box 6: Breda, Netherlands—2019 Access City Award Winner

This beautiful medieval city made a special effort to make the historical center accessible. The majority of sports facilities, museums, theaters, and community centers in the city have been improved to accommodate persons with disabilities.

The city created an accessibility fund to help organizations with communications and to fund small physical improvements including for events. The city raises awareness of disability among business owners and has checked the accessibility of more than 800 shops and restaurants.

The municipal website is accessible, and the city also tested and improved the 25 main websites used for communicating with citizens.

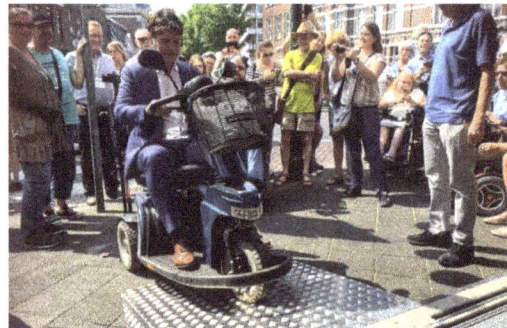

Shops, restaurants and organized events in Breda made improvements for persons with disabilities.
Source: European Commission Access City Awards.

Box 7: Lyon, France—2018 Access City Award Winner

The city won the award for making accessibility a central element of its local development plan showing that accessibility benefits everyone in the city.

The public buses are accessible and so is access to culture through inclusion of accessible equipment in libraries, such as reading machines, audiobook readers, and magnifying screens. Digital tools are available to promote the mobility and participation of persons with disabilities.

Lyon is also a model in promoting inclusion at work; 7.8% of its civil servants have a disability, well above the national average.

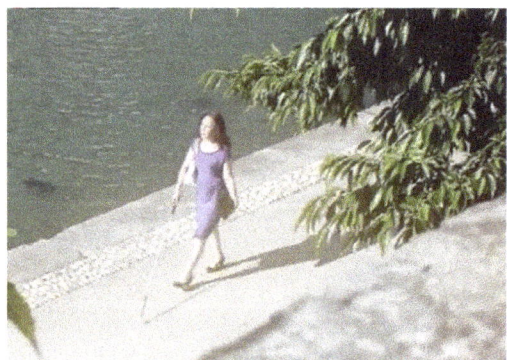

Accessibility in public transport and pathways found in Lyon.
Source: European Commission Access City Awards.

Box 8: Chester, United Kingdom—2017 Access City Award Winner

With a population of 329,000, about 18% of the residents of Chester have a disability, with 21% aged over 65. The city has employed an access officer since 1991.

All the historical sites in the city are accessible. The city promotes participation in city life by providing a large number of accessible parking spaces for persons with disabilities. Chester also enables the elderly and persons with disabilities to hire a wheelchair or scooter to help them access the shopping areas.

All information is available in alternative formats. An online directory of services provides a wide range of information, including details on accessibility, public transport, and car parking.

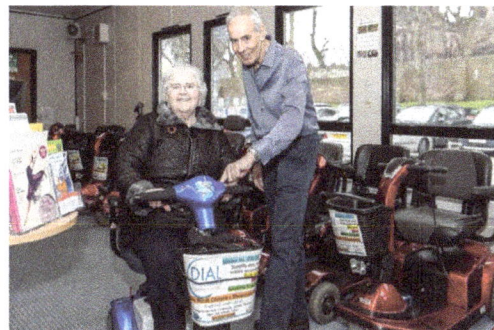

Elderly and persons with disabilities benefit from accessible parking in Chester.
Source: European Commission Access City Awards.

Accessible Heritage Sites, Monuments, Outdoor Environments, and Buildings in Georgia

City of Mtskheta

A significant part of the establishment of the state of Georgia is associated with Mtskheta, the country's historical city and former capital. The city is rich with historical monuments, such as Svetitskhoveli Cathedral, which is under the protection of the United Nations Educational, Scientific and Cultural Organization. Mtskheta is one of the most important tourist destinations, famous for its ancient historical center and restaurants offering traditional Georgian cuisine. Tourism is the key source of income for the local population of about 7,000.

The city of Mtskheta. Aerial view of the city of Mtskheta (photo by PARSA).

In Mtskheta, accessibility improvement projects are taking place at four historical monuments:

- Svetitskhoveli Cathedral

- Samtavro Monastery
- Mtskheta St. Stephen's Church Antioquia
- Shiomghvime Monastery and tourism information center.

These are being carried out according to universal design principles and international and local accessibility standards by architects and access audit specialists of the Accessible Tourism Centre (PARSA). The Ministry of Economy and Sustainable Development of Georgia and the Georgian National Tourism Administration provide funding and support for the accessibility improvement projects.

Works conducted. First, an access audit was carried out to identify a systematic approach to the planning and delivery of the projects. The goal of the access audit researchers and architects was to ensure compliance with universal design and international and local accessibility standards while having minimal intrusion to the historic fabric of the monuments.

Detectable warning strips. One example of a universal design intervention is the application of detectable warning surfaces with contrasting colors at the head and foot of stairs adjacent to the cathedrals to support people with a visual impairment.

Detectable warnings and surfaces for the blind and vision impairment people. Accessibility project of historical center of city of Mtskheta (photos by PARSA and Georgian National Tourism Administration).

Ramps. Another example of a universal design intervention is the provision of ramps to overcome level differences previously only possible via stairs. The materials used and construction of the permanent ramps are in harmony with the facade of the historical center. Some of the ramps are removable to offer access while not interfering with the historic fabric of the monuments.

Ramps for wheelchair users. Accessibility project of historical center of city of Mtskheta (photos by PARSA).

Elevators. In places where it was impossible to install ramps because they would damage the facade of the historical monument, an external elevator was installed. The elevator is self-supported and does not touch the walls. It is adapted to the needs of wheelchair users as well as for the blind and persons with vision impairment.

Platform lift for persons with disabilities. Accessibility project of historical center of city of Mtskheta (photos by PARSA, Georgian National Tourism Administration and Michel Marang).

Accessible information. Tactile scale models of all the monuments were created to support people with a visual impairment. Each is a precise copy of the monument. To make them more realistic, the architects of the PARSA created the models from the same stone used to build the monuments. Information boards in several languages and braille are installed beside the models.

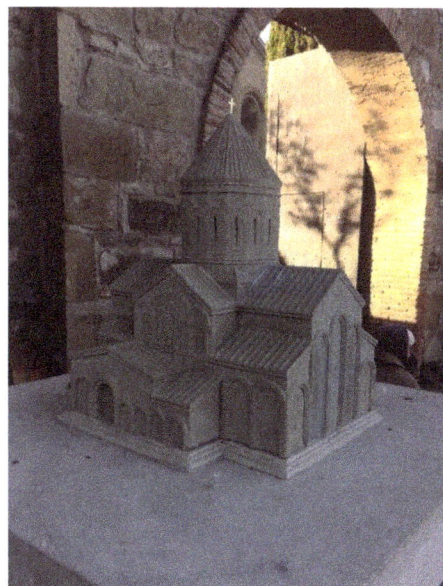

Tactile models of historical monument for persons that are blind and with vision impairment. Accessibility project of historical center of city of Mtskheta (photos by PARSA).

Tactile model of historical monument for blind and vision impairment people.
Accessibility project of historical center of city of Mtskheta (photo by Michel Marang).

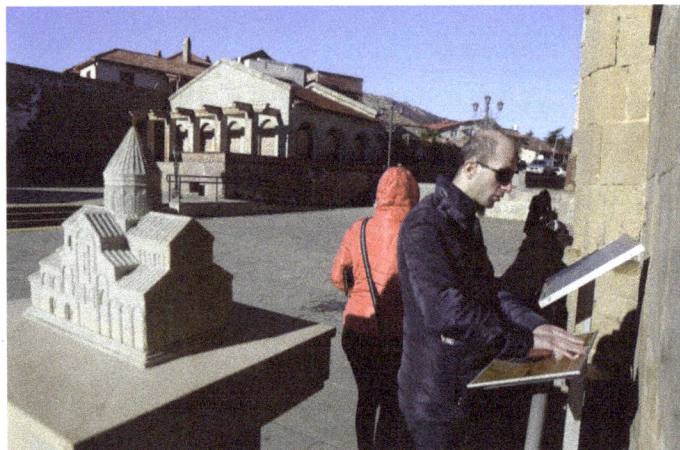

Tactile model and information of historical monument in braille for blind and vision impairment people. (photo by Georgian National Tourism Administration).

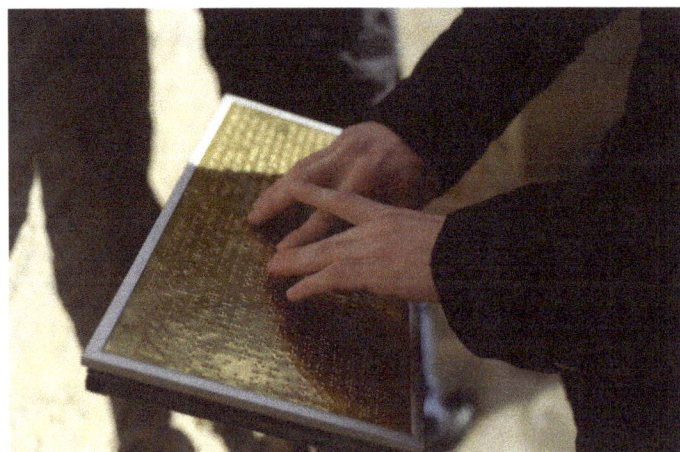

Information of historical monument in braille for persons that are blind.
Accessibility project of historical center of city of Mtskheta (photo by Georgian National Tourism Administration).

Tskaltubo Central Park

Tskaltubo, located in the central part of west Georgia, is known for its therapeutic thermal baths and beautiful Central Park. The spa resorts located around the Central Park make Tskaltubo a very important tourist destination.

In Tskaltubo, accessibility projects have also been carried out by architects and access audit specialists of the PARSA in accordance with universal design and international and local accessibility standards. Funding and support here have also been provided by the Ministry of Economy and Sustainable Development of Georgia and the Georgian National Tourism Administration.

Works conducted. First, an access audit was carried out to identify a systematic approach to the planning and delivery of the project. The goal of the access audit researchers and architects was to ensure compliance with universal design and international and local accessibility standards. The access audit informed the planning of an accessible route system in the park to cover all facilities that the Central Park offers, including the Cold Lake area, the park entrances, streets around the park, car parking, and crossroads.

Central Park and Cold Lake. New accessible routes were provided across the Central Park and Cold Lake area. Wheelchair users and other mobility aid users can now reach all important points, including the Bungalow Bar, toilet facilities, the decorative pool, piers, cafés, and the sports complex, without encountering any obstacles.

Accessible routes. The city of Tskaltubo: Accessibility project of Tskaltubo central park (photos by Georgian National Tourism Administration).

Bungalow Bar. Making all the facilities and services at the Bungalow Bar accessible for everyone is important, including for persons with disabilities. Previously, there was no level access to the bar; access was by stairs only. The bar has now a new ramp designed in an empathetic way, echoing the round shape of the Bungalow Bar and blending with the existing design and environment.

Access to the Bungalow Bar, ramps. The city of Tskaltubo: Accessibility project of Tskaltubo central park (photo by Georgian National Tourism Administration).

The Piers. To provide level access to the piers, a 21-meter ramp was constructed with regular level landings. The materials, construction, and design of the ramp are in harmony with the surrounding environment. This project also included recommendations on how to make the existing boat trip service accessible for wheelchair users by using accessible boat lifts.

Access to the Piers, ramp. The city of Tskaltubo: Accessibility project of Tskaltubo central park (photos by Georgian National Tourism Administration).

Georgian Parliament Building in Tbilisi

Georgia's historical Parliament building on Rustaveli Avenue in Tbilisi, built between 1938 and 1953, is one of the most important architectural and historical buildings in the country.

A project to improve accessibility according to universal design and international and local accessibility standards was carried out by architects and access audit specialists from the PARSA with funding and support from the Parliament of Georgia.

Works conducted. An access audit was carried out to identify a systematic approach to the planning and delivery of the project. The goal of the access audit researchers and architects was to ensure compliance with universal design and international and local accessibility standards. The access audit also helped ensure there was minimal damage to the historic fabric of the monument. Work accomplished includes provision of the following:

- accessible arrival parking areas;
- accessible routes to the entrances;
- accessible lifts at the entrances;
- automatic door systems;
- an accessible reception;
- assistive technical equipment;
- a tactile paving system with detectable warning surfaces, signage, and wayfinding;
- accessible toilet facilities;
- accessible routes, including ramps and platform lifts;
- navigation and orientation systems for persons that are blind and with vision impairment; and
- tactile models and maps.

Curb ramp and platform lifts at the entrance. Georgian Parliament Building in Tbilisi: Accessibility project of Georgian Parliament Building (photo by PARSA).

Platform lift at the entrance. Georgian Parliament Building in Tbilisi: Accessibility project of Georgian Parliament Building (photo by PARSA).

Platform lift at the entrance. Georgian Parliament Building in Tbilisi: Accessibility project of Georgian Parliament Building (photo by PARSA).

Platform lift at the entrance. Georgian Parliament Building in Tbilisi: Accessibility project of Georgian Parliament Building (photo by Nino Zedginidze / UNDP, The Parliament of Georgia).

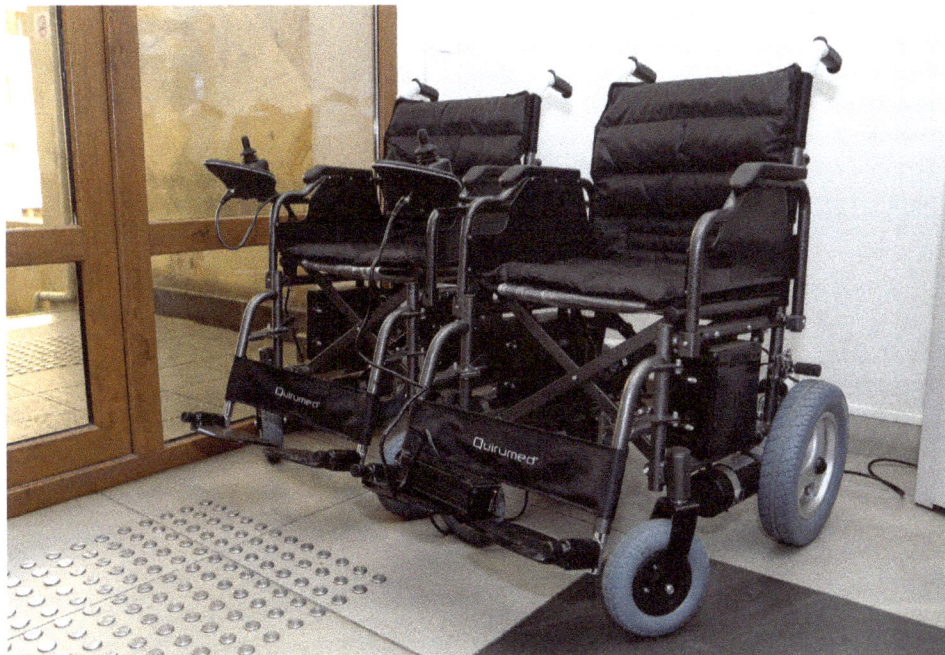

Wheelchairs for persons with disabilities. Georgian Parliament Building in Tbilisi: Accessibility project of Georgian Parliament Building (photo by Nino Zedginidze / UNDP, The Parliament of Georgia).

Evacuation chair for persons with disabilities. Georgian Parliament Building in Tbilisi: Accessibility project of Georgian Parliament Building (photo by Nino Zedginidze / UNDP, The Parliament of Georgia).

Interior platform lift for wheelchair users. Georgian Parliament Building in Tbilisi: Accessibility project of Georgian Parliament Building (photo by PARSA).

Case Study—Application of the National Accessibility Standards

"M Square" Affordable Housing Project, Tbilisi, Georgia

An accessibility audit applying the "National Accessibility Standards" was conducted under the Livable Cities Investment Project for Balanced Development on the design of a private sector development for affordable social housing in Tbilisi Georgia called "M Square."

The M Square project is supported by the private sector operations department of the Asian Development Bank (ADB). Collaboration and support from ADB to the responsible private development company, "m²" included delivering the main findings from the accessibility audit survey; and providing recommendations, consultations, and site visits. The intention being to help improve the accessibility of the development according to the principals of inclusive design and in accordance with relevant international and local accessibility legislation, regulations, and standards, including the newly approved National Accessibility Standards (as set out in this document).

The accessibility audit included a detailed review of architectural drawings for the development against the new Standards with key recommendations targeting the detailed design of accessible parking spaces, ramps, access routes and detectable warning surfaces, signage, and emergency evacuation. This process supports the progress of inclusive developments by sharing knowledge, technical expertise, and piloting the successful implementation of the Standards.

The development company m² has a social responsibility strategy in place that aims to create a comfortable, accessible, and safe environment for all its residents. Together with Tbilisi City Hall, m² contributes to the well-being of 2,500 affected residents of suspended housing construction projects in Tbilisi including Chkhondideli Str./Nadzaladevi District, Mirtkhulava Str./Didube District, and other locations.

It is expected that the M Square affordable housing project, with support from ADB, becomes an exemplar for comfortable, accessible, and safe affordable housing development for the city of Tbilisi and Georgia more generally.

Image Copyright: m² Development.

5 CONCLUSION

Inclusive Cities: Urban Area Guidelines provides a comprehensive overview of the need and demand for the creation of inclusive cities around the world and in Georgia. The benefits are many, not just for all Georgia's citizens, but also for a wider range of visitors to the country, in turn supporting the significant tourism industry. This is important for the economy and for Georgia's international recognition as a welcoming and caring nation.

Georgia's current approach to delivering inclusive cities has been clearly set out against the international context, driven by the country's commitment to meet the United Nations Convention on the Rights of Persons with Disabilities (UNCRPD). While inclusion covers a wide range of sectors and groups from gender to the elderly and children, the focus of these guidelines has been persons with disabilities (PWDs). It is widely accepted that considering the needs of PWDs from the very start and throughout the development of a project helps deliver better outcomes that support everyone, not just persons with disabilities. This is a key principle of universal design.

The universal design standards provided here are those mandated by the Government of Georgia as being applicable to all development projects. They are derived from the Resolution 732 on Technical Regulation: National Accessibility Standards and are a good benchmark from which to build on. It is important that these are viewed as the minimum acceptable standard for development projects and not an aspiration. A good universal design will always strive to do more and deliver the best and most inclusive designs and outcomes possible. It is also important to always consult and engage with end users, including persons with disabilities. Involving persons with disabilities throughout the design process will support more informed outcomes and, in many cases, can result in more innovative solutions based on collaboration and a better understanding of the real issues.

Finally, the case studies and examples provided demonstrate that a lot of good work is already happening in Georgia and around the world to deliver inclusive design solutions as well as inclusive and more livable cities. The benefits of this work must be recognized to ensure it is continued as Georgia evolves to become a more inclusive and accessible place to both live and visit.

The journey toward an inclusive city has started. Embedding the universal design principles and guidance contained in this publication can help ensure the journey continues—helping create a more inclusive, accessible, and prosperous future for Georgia and the Central and West Asia region.

REFERENCES

Administration of the Government of Georgia. 2020. Georgia Voluntary National Review: Report on the Implementation of the 2030 Agenda on Sustainable Development.

Asian Development Bank. 2016. *Realizing the Urban Potential in Georgia: National Urban Assessment*. *Executive Summary*. Manila.

Asian Development Bank. 2019. *Future Cities, Future Women Initiative: Phase 1*. Final Report. Manila.

Asian Development Bank. 2019. *Guidance Note on Stakeholder Communication Strategies for Projects in South Asia*.

Asian Development Bank. 2019. *Strategy 2030 Operational Plan for Priority 4: Making Cities More Livable, 2019–2024*. Manila.

Baker, M. 1989. *Tourism for All: A Report of the Working Party Chaired by Mary Baker*. London: English Tourist Board in association with the Holiday Care Service, the Scottish Tourist Board, the Wales Tourist Board.

Brault, M. 2012. Americans with Disabilities: 2010 Household Economic Studies. *Current Population Reports*.

Carroll, A. and A. Buchholtz. 2012. *Business and Society: Ethics, Sustainability, and Stakeholder Management*. Stanford. p. 88.

Chaplin, D., J. Twigg, and E. Lovell. 2019. Intersectional Approaches to Vulnerability Reduction and Resilience Building: A Scoping Study. *Resilience Intel*. London: BRACED and ODI.

Clarkson, P.J. and R. Coleman. 2013. History of Inclusive Design in the UK. *Applied Ergonomics*. http:// dx.doi.org/10.1016/j.apergo.2013.03.002

Center for Disease Control and Prevention. Disability Impacts All of Us (infographic).

Disability Inclusive and Accessible Urban Development Network (DIAUD), World Enabled, and CBM. 2016. *The Inclusion Imperative: Towards Disability-Inclusive and Accessible Urban Development*. Key Recommendations for an Inclusive Urban Agenda. p.13.

European Commission. Access City Awards.

European Commission. 2010. European Disability Strategy 2010–2020: A Renewed Commitment to a Barrier-Free Europe.

European Commission. 2012. Economic Impact and Travel Patterns of Accessible Tourism in Europe: Final Report.

European Commission, Horizon 2020 Programme. *The EU Framework Programme for Research and Innovation*.

European Network for Accessible Tourism. 2010. *A Europe Accessible for All*. (Report from expert group set up by the European Commission).

European Network for Accessible Tourism. 2014. *Mind the Accessibility Gap: Proceedings of the European Conference*. Brussels.

Fletcher, G. et al. 2003. Mapping Stakeholder Perceptions for a Third Sector Organization. *Pike Journal of Intellectual Capital*. 1 December.

Georgian National Tourism Administration. 2015. Georgian Tourism in Figures: Structure and Industry Data.

Global Disability Innovation Hub, Queen Elizabeth Olympic Park, and London Legacy Development Corporation. 2019. Inclusive Design Standards.

Government of Georgia. 2016. National Regulation Decree No. 41: Technical Regulations for the Safety Rules for Buildings.

Government of Georgia. 2020. Resolution 732 on Technical Regulation: National Accessibility Standards. Tblisi

Government of Ireland, National Disability Authority. 2011. *Access: Improving the Accessibility of Historic Building and Places*. Dublin. p. 16.

Infrastructure and Cities for Economic Development (ICED). 2019. *Delivering Disability Inclusive Infrastructure in Low Income Countries*.

Institute for the Development of Freedom of Information. 2018. Data Analysis on Persons with Disabilities Living in Georgia.

International Code Council Inc. 2017. Standard for Accessible and Usable Buildings and Facilities. ICC-A117.-2017.

IONESCO, Icomos France. 2013. *Heritage and Accessibility: How to Make Protected Towns, Monuments and Sites in Europe*. European Symposium. 21–22 March.

Krishnamurthy, S. et al. 2011. Child-Friendly Urban Design: Observations on Public Space from Eindhoven (NL) and Jerusalem (IL). Bernard van Leer Foundation.

Macel, R. 1985. "Universal design, barrier-free environments for everyone". Los Angeles: *Designers West* 33(1). pp. 147–152

Mitchell, R. and D. Wood. 1997. Toward a Theory of Stakeholder Identification and Salience: Defining the Principle of Who and What Really Counts. *The Academy of Management Review.* 22(4). pp. 853–886.

Mitlin, D. and D. Satterthwaite. 2016. *On the Engagement of Excluded Groups in Inclusive Cities: Highlighting Good Practices and Key Challenges in the Global South.* Urban Development Series Knowledge Papers. Washington, DC: World Bank.

Naik Singru, R. and M. Lindfield. 2017. *Enabling Inclusive Cities: Tool Kit for Inclusive Urban Development.* Manila.

National Statistics Office of Georgia and Georgian National Tourism Administration.

OECD Council on SDGs. 2019. *Gender Equality and Sustainable Infrastructure.*

Parliament of Georgia. 2014. Law of Georgia on the Elimination of All Forms of Discrimination.

Patrick, M., I. McKinnon, and V. Austin. 2020. Inclusive Design and Accessibility in Ulaanbaatar, Mongolia. *AT2030 Inclusive Infrastructure Case Studies.* Prepared by the Global Disability Innovation Hub and partners for the UK Foreign, Commonwealth and Development Office.

Pinilla-Roncancio, M. and S. Alkire. 2017. How Poor are People with Disabilities? Evidence Based on the Global Multidimensional Poverty Index. *Journal of Disability Policy Studies.*

Rodney, J.R., K.V. Grude, and L. Thurloway. 1996. *The Project Manager as Change Agent: Leadership, Influence and Negotiation.* London: McGraw-Hill.

Savage, G.T. et al. 1991. Strategies for Assessing and Managing Organizational Stakeholders. *The Executive.* 5(2). pp. 61–75.

Smart Tourism Capital. Helsinki: Taking Smart to New Heights.

Steinfeld, E. and J. Maisel. 2012. *Universal Design: Creating Inclusive Environments.* United States: Center for Inclusive Design and Environmental Access (IDeA).

Tanadgoma. 2007. *Library—Cultural Center for People with Disabilities "Tanadgoma."*

The American Society of Mechanical Engineers. 2016. *Safety Code for Elevators and Escalators.* ASME A17.1/CSA B44 Handbook: ASME A17.1-2016; *Safety Code for Elevators.* CSA B44-16.

The American Society of Mechanical Engineers. 2008. *Safety Standard for Platform Lifts and Stair Chairlifts* ASME A18.1.

The Clarkson Center for Business Ethics, Joseph L. Rotman School of Management, University of Toronto. 1999. *Principles of Stakeholder Management.* Toronto.

The Institute for Human Centered Design.

UNICEF. 2004. *Building Child Friendly Cities: A Framework for Action*.

UNICEF. 2012. Towards Cities Fit for Children. The State of the World's Children.

UN Habitat. Inclusive, Vibrant Neighbourhoods and Communities.

United Nations Human Settlements Programme. 2007. *Inclusive and Sustainable Urban Planning: A Guide for Municipalities.*

United Nations. Convention on the Rights of Persons with Disabilities (CRPD).

United Nations. 2016. *Disability and Sustainable Urban Development (Infographic)*.

United Nations Office of the High Commissioner for Human Rights. Convention on the Rights of Persons with Disabilities.

United Nations. Sustainable Development Goals.

United Nations Sustainable Development Group. 2016. *The Sustainable Development Goals are Coming to Life—Stories of Country Implementation and UN Support*.

United Nations World Tourism Organization. Accessible Tourism.

United Nations World Tourism Organization. Global Code of Ethics for Tourism.

UN-WOMEN. 2011. *Building Safe and Inclusive Cities for Woman: A Practical Guide*.

Urban Development. 2013. *Gender Mainstreaming in Urban Planning and Urban Development*. Vienna.

VisitBritain. Great Britain Tour Survey.

World Accessibility Initiative. World Content Accessibility Guidelines (WCAG).

World Bank. 2015. *World Inclusive Cities Approach Paper*.

World Bank and Kounkuey Design Initiative. 2020. *Handbook for Gender-Inclusive Urban Planning Design*. Washington, DC.

World Health Organization. *Measuring the Age-Friendliness of Cities: A Guide to Using Core Indicators*.

World Health Organization. 2007. *Checklist of Essential Features of Age-friendly Cities*.

World Health Organization. The WHO Age-friendly Cities Framework.

World Health Organization. 2011. World Report on Disability 2011.

www.ingramcontent.com/pod-product-compliance
Lightning Source LLC
Chambersburg PA
CBHW061235270326
41929CB00031B/3495

Inclusive Cities
Urban Area Guidelines

Cities in Asia and the Pacific are expanding rapidly. With this growth, persons with disabilities, older persons, women, and children face significant challenges in accessing urban services and fully participating in city life. To address such barriers, inclusive environments are needed wherein infrastructure and services are built considering the different needs of everyone. The inclusive cities guidelines provide universal design solutions, accessibility standards, and case studies on inclusive urban development to help create a barrier-free built environment and public space. These guidelines adopt both international standards and national standards in Georgia to provide support to urban practitioners and planners in ensuring old and new developments can adapt and contribute toward the creation of inclusive and livable cities.

About the Asian Development Bank

ADB is committed to achieving a prosperous, inclusive, resilient, and sustainable Asia and the Pacific, while sustaining its efforts to eradicate extreme poverty. Established in 1966, it is owned by 68 members —49 from the region. Its main instruments for helping its developing member countries are policy dialogue, loans, equity investments, guarantees, grants, and technical assistance.

ISBN 978-92-9269-316-9

ASIAN DEVELOPMENT BANK
6 ADB Avenue, Mandaluyong City
1550 Metro Manila, Philippines
www.adb.org

9 789292 693169

INNOVATIVE FINANCE APPROACHES FOR ADDRESSING RIVER BASIN POLLUTION
COMBATING AQUATIC BIODIVERSITY LOSS IN SOUTHEAST ASIA

JUNE 2024

ACGF
ASEAN CATALYTIC GREEN FINANCE FACILITY

ADB